DISCOVERING U.S. HISTORY

The Great Depression

1929–1938

DISCOVERING U.S. HISTORY

The New World: Prehistory–1542

Colonial America: 1543–1763

Revolutionary America: 1764–1789

Early National America: 1790–1850

The Civil War Era: 1851–1865

The New South and the Old West: 1866–1890

The Gilded Age and Progressivism: 1891–1913

World War I and the Roaring Twenties: 1914–1928

The Great Depression: 1929–1938

World War II: 1939–1945

The Cold War and Postwar America: 1946–1963

Modern America: 1964–Present

DISCOVERING U.S. HISTORY

The Great Depression
1929–1938

Tim McNeese

Consulting Editor: Richard Jensen, Ph.D.

CHELSEA HOUSE
PUBLISHERS
An imprint of Infobase Publishing

THE GREAT DEPRESSION: 1929–1938

Chelsea House
An imprint of Infobase Publishing
132 West 31st Street
New York NY 10001

Library of Congress Cataloging-in-Publication Data
McNeese, Tim.
  The Great Depression, 1929–1938 / by Tim McNeese.
      p. cm. — (Discovering U.S. history)
  Includes bibliographical references and index.
  ISBN 978-1-60413-357-8 (hardcover)
  1. United States—History—1933–1945—Juvenile literature. 2. Depressions—1929—United States—
Juvenile literature. 3. United States—History—1919–1933—Juvenile literature. 4. United States—
Economic conditions—1918–1945—Juvenile literature. 5. Economic history—1918–1945—Juvenile
literature. 6. World politics—1933–1945—Juvenile literature. I. Title. II. Series.

  E806.M47 2009
  973.917—dc22

                                   2009022090

Chelsea House books are available at special discounts when purchased in
bulk quantities for businesses, associations, institutions, or sales promotions.
Please call our Special Sales Department in New York at (212) 967-8800
or (800) 322-8755.

You can find Chelsea House on the World Wide Web at http://www.chelseahouse.com

The Discovering U.S. History series was produced for Chelsea House by
Bender Richardson White, Uxbridge, UK

Editors: Lionel Bender and Susan Malyan
Designer and Picture Researcher: Ben White
Production: Kim Richardson
Maps and graphics: Stefan Chabluk

Cover printed by Bang Printing, Brainerd, MN
Book printed and bound by Bang Printing, Brainerd, MN
Date printed: April 2010
Printed in the United States of America

This book is printed on acid-free paper.

All links and web addresses were checked and verified to be correct at the time of publication. Because of
the dynamic nature of the web, some addresses and links may have changed since publication and may no
longer be valid.

Contents

Introduction

The Bonus March

In the early summer of 1931, 3 million veterans of World War I (1914–18) watched anxiously as a committee considered their immediate futures. That June a committee of the House of Representatives was holding a hearing concerning an extremely controversial subject: Whether to pay a bonus to U.S. servicemen who had been in uniform during World War I.

Congress had established the Soldiers Bonus Act in 1924 with good intentions. The act's Adjusted Compensation Certificates were intended to serve as a combined form of pension and life insurance policy, but they were not to be paid until 1945, when many of the veterans of World War I would be approaching their late 40s or early 50s. The only exceptions to receiving the bonus sooner were the heirs of any vets who had already died. Many vets, however, now wanted the bonus early. In fact, many of them were relying on it as their only income.

For nearly two years, the United States had been struggling with a severe economic depression. Millions of Americans were out of work; businesses and factories had closed by the thousands, along with hundreds of banks. The veterans and their families were desperate. The planned bonus would mean $1,000 per wartime serviceman, totaling $3 billion. If Congress paid out the bonus that year, in the midst of the Depression, it would translate into the largest direct relief program for the poor in the history of the federal government.

A STACKED DECK

Veterans were summoned to testify at the House Committee hearings, but many believed the deck was stacked against them. President Herbert Hoover, a conservative Republican, did not support the bonus. Nor did a host of committee witnesses, including bank officials, insurance executives, and a field of business people. There were a few sympathetic congressmen, as well as a handful of veteran organization officials, who favored paying out the bonus that year. However, despite the number of opponents of the immediate bonus payout, much of their testimony was boring, laden with charts and statistics. The veterans gave the most compelling testimony, particularly one out-of-work vet from New Jersey who had walked from the city of Camden to the Capitol just to tell his story.

One Veteran Speaks

Appearing before the committee, Joseph Angelo spoke directly to his need:

> *All I ask of you, brothers, is to help us. We helped you, now you help us. My partner here has a wife and five children, and he is just the same as I am. He hiked down here at*

the same time with me, and our feet are blistered. That is all I have to say. And I hope you folks can help us and that we can go through with the bonus. We don't want charity; we don't need it. All we ask for is what belongs to us, and that is all we want.

Intrigued congressmen asked Angelo about the medal he was wearing. "I carry the highest medal in America for enlisted men," he answered, "the Distinguished Service Cross." He had gained it by rescuing an officer during a machine gun attack in France's Argonne Forest in 1918. Nearly all of Angelo's unit had been killed, but he survived and rescued the wounded colonel. Angelo then showed the committee members a tie tack that had been fashioned from one of the bullets removed from the American officer's leg. He explained that his medal and the tie pin were the only two personal items he still owned. The rest he had been forced by his circumstances to sell in a pawnshop back in Camden.

Hard Times for Americans

Here before the House Committee was a man who had served his country, but who had fallen on hard times, like millions of other veterans and tens of millions of other Americans. In 1929 the United States had begun to slide into a deep economic depression that in 1931 had not yet even reached bottom. The working class had become restless. That summer at least 5 million men and women in America had no jobs, while another 5 million were only partially employed. Since the stock market crash in October 1929 nearly one in every two U.S. workers had faced wage cuts. Poverty had become a new way of life for America's millions.

The country's bad times had already driven 2 million vets to "borrow" against their bonuses. But for every $100 taken out to pay for an immediate need, the veterans needed much more than that. If they waited until 1945, their bonuses would be greater than the $1,000 they were now asking for, but, given the difficulties they were facing, many of those former servicemen were uncertain they would live long enough to receive it. They had found a congressman who cared, Representative Wright Patman from Texas. He had now introduced a bill that would authorize the U.S. Treasury to print $2.5 billion in new money to pay off the veterans' bonuses.

THE MARCHERS SET UP CAMP

To provide a voice of support for the bill that many veterans considered so crucial to their futures, thousands of them had made the trip to Washington, D.C. They began arriving in the city the following November, hopping freight trains or walking great distances. They soon called themselves the Bonus Expeditionary Force, a reminder of their war days when they served as members of the AEF—the American Expeditionary Force.

When they reached Washington the veterans found shelter where they could. President Hoover appointed General Pelham D. Glassford, the youngest American brigadier general of World War I, as superintendent of Washington's police force. Glassford became sympathetic to the Bonus Marchers and found them quarters in unoccupied buildings along Pennsylvania Avenue, between the Capitol and the White House.

However, so many veterans showed up that Glassford had to set up another location for them, a campsite at a low-lying landfill where the Potomac and Anacostia Rivers joined, known as Anacostia Flats. He made building materials available to them, including lumber and boxes of nails, and arranged for food to be provided by the Salvation Army, American Legion Posts, and local Washington citizens. Glassford rode out regularly on his blue motorcycle to visit the camp, and he paid $773 out of his own pocket to provide food for the veterans. By early June, 1932, the Anacostia Flats camp numbered 7,000 men, with most of them living in makeshift wooden shacks.

The Marchers created their own temporary city. With bathroom facilities unavailable, the vets went over to some of the Smithsonian museums to use theirs. Frank Taylor, who was serving as a junior curator in the Arts and Industries Building (by the 1960s, he had become the founding director of the National Museum of American History), later remembered, notes historian Paul Dickson: "They were very orderly and came in to use the rest room. We did ask that they not do any bathing or shaving before the museum opened." The camps were run with military proficiency. One observer recalled: "They had their own M.P.s [Military Police] and officers in charge, and flag raising ceremonies, complete with a fellow playing bugle."

A SETBACK, BUT THE FIGHT GOES ON
As the House prepared to vote on the Patman bonus bill in mid-June, 15,000 Bonus Marchers engaged in a march through downtown Washington toward the Capitol. They marched rank and file, just as they had during their days in the military. Tens of thousands of locals came out in support, lining the route of the Bonus Marchers.

On June 17 the Senate prepared to vote on the bill, and the chamber gallery was filled with veterans. Senators in support of the bill said the bonus would be paid in 13 years anyway, so why not pay out now, when people really needed the money? Others argued against the bill, saying that millions of non-veterans needed help just as badly. At 8 P.M. the Senate vote was taken, and the bill lost by a vote of 62 to 18. This was a crushing blow for the Bonus Marchers.

Outside, 10,000 veterans were gathered, waiting. When one of their leaders emerged from the Capitol and announced

The Bonus Army gathers outside the Capitol in June 1932. The World War I veterans demanded that Congress authorize payment of war bonuses. The police and army eventually dispersed the veterans.

the bill's defeat, there was both anger and disappointment. Some talked of rioting, but they were soon calmed by their former comrades, who told them to go back to their encampments. The fight for the bonus would continue, one shouted, until they all got what they had come for.

A FINAL CONFRONTATION

The Bonus Army did not leave the city. In fact, during the weeks that followed even more veterans showed up to add their support. Their numbers became difficult to estimate; perhaps 20,000, even 50,000, by July. But the bill was dead, and no amount of veterans living in a shantytown outside Washington was going to change that. The government did respond to the continuing presence of the Bonus Marchers, offering to pay their ways home with train fare or gasoline, plus 75 cents a day for any other expenses. Thousands accepted the offer, but thousands more would not give up or leave.

On July 16, as Congress was preparing to adjourn, the Bonus Marchers once again marched on the Capitol, a force 7,000 strong. There a frustrated Glassford ordered the arrest of the marchers' leader, Walter Waters. Only after several congressmen came out and intervened was the situation defused. Waters was released, and the army of angry Bonus Marchers dispersed. However, a large-scale confrontation was about to break to the surface.

On July 28 that break opened up when Glassford ordered the D. C. police out to Anacostia Flats to close down the makeshift encampment and send the veterans home. President Hoover had tired of them and did not intend to negotiate with them in any way. There was angry resistance, which led to a riot, and two Bonus Marchers were killed. Hoover then ordered federal troops, under the command of the army's Chief of Staff, General Douglas MacArthur, to march out to Anacostia Flats, secure the shantytown, and contain the rioting veterans.

The Veterans Move Out

It was a curious and sad scene that unfolded as active U.S. Army soldiers, numbering more than 1,000 and armed with bayoneted rifles and blue canisters of tear gas, marched on their former comrades. MacArthur ordered up a machine-gun squadron and mounted cavalrymen with sabers drawn. There were even a half dozen tanks. By 4 P.M., the Bonus Marchers had been driven out at the point of a bayonet and in a cloud of tear gas. They did not fight back. They tried to hang on to their shacks, and they cursed at the soldiers, but they obeyed.

Their dreams of a much-needed bonus put to rest, the veterans packed up and moved out of Anacostia Flats. Once they abandoned their shanties, MacArthur ordered the buildings burned. One of those who watched his shack burn that late afternoon was Joe Angelo. As he blinked back the burning caused by the tear gas, Angelo recognized one of the officers barking out orders to his men. He was the colonel Angelo had rescued in the Argonne Forest 14 years earlier, a cavalry officer named George S. Patton, who would one day become the greatest tank commander of World War II.

A NEW DEAL IN SIGHT?

As thousands of veterans abandoned hope that day in Washington, the nation stood at its own brink. For nearly three years millions had struggled through the Great Depression with no relief in sight. Their only hope lay in 1932 being an election year. The Democratic candidate, a New Yorker named Franklin Delano Roosevelt, was making promises. Just a few weeks earlier, at the Democratic Party convention, Roosevelt had been handed his party's nomination for president. There on the convention floor Roosevelt had said: "I pledge you, I pledge myself to a new deal for the American people." Certainly the Bonus Marchers had not received the deal they had been looking for. Could the election offer an alternative to the conservative Hoover? Might the future hold greater promise? Could the answers to the problems of the Depression actually be only a vote away?

The New Deal and Dust Bowl

The New Deal was a government program to overcome the Depression. It was based on three Rs—Relief, Recovery, and Reform. It prompted the construction of highways across the country and built new dams that produced electricity. Its success was tempered by the Dust Bowl, which damaged the prairies and slowed recovery.

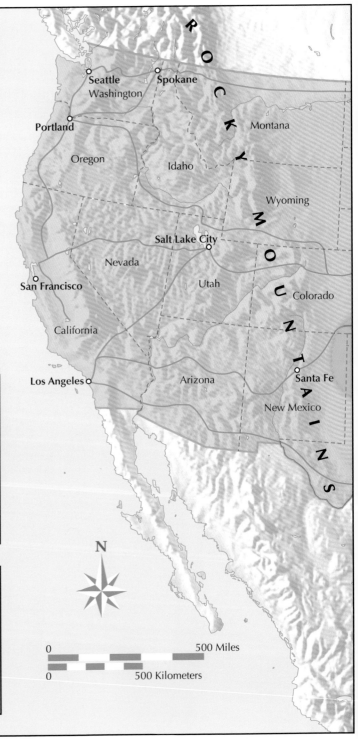

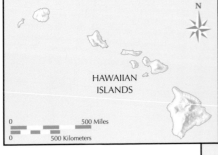

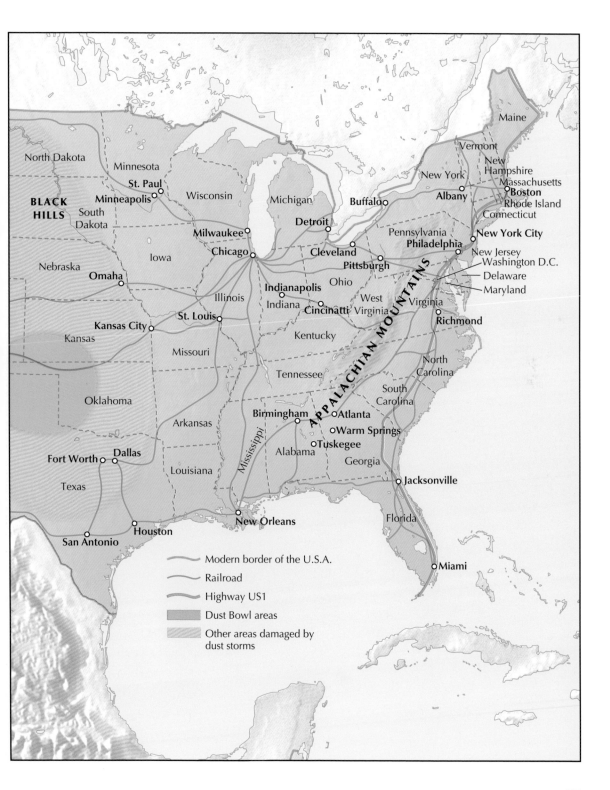

North Dakota

Minnesota

St. Paul

Minneapolis

**BLACK
HILLS**

South
Dakota

Wisconsin

Michigan

Buffalo

New York

Albany

Maine

Vermont

New
Hampshire

Massachusetts

Boston

Rhode Island

Connecticut

Milwaukee

Detroit

Pennsylvania

New York City

Philadelphia

Chicago

Cleveland

Pittsburgh

New Jersey

Washington D.C.

Delaware

Maryland

Nebraska

Omaha

Iowa

Illinois

Indianapolis

Indiana

Ohio

Cincinatti

West
Virginia

Virginia

Richmond

St. Louis

Kansas City

Kansas

Missouri

Kentucky

Tennessee

North
Carolina

Oklahoma

Arkansas

South
Carolina

Birmingham

Atlanta

Warm Springs

Tuskegee

Alabama

Georgia

Jacksonville

Fort Worth

Dallas

Louisiana

Texas

Mississippi

San Antonio

Houston

New Orleans

Florida

Miami

APPALACHIAN MOUNTAINS

Modern border of the U.S.A.

Railroad

Highway US1

Dust Bowl areas

Other areas damaged by
dust storms

1

A Deceptive Economy

In 1928, after eight years of conservative Republican leadership, a generally contented American public stayed the course and elected a third such president. Overall, life in the United States had been good for many Americans, as the nation's prosperity hit a stride that many people could not imagine ending. Some had even come to believe that the U.S. economy had fallen into an endless groove of permanent growth. The new president certainly seemed to think so. While still the Republican candidate, Herbert Hoover, who had served the Coolidge administration as secretary of commerce, gave a speech in August touting the great strides already made by a national economy on the rise: "We in America today are nearer to the final triumph over poverty than ever before in the history of any land. The poorhouse is vanishing from among us."

In the fall of 1928 such words seemed to ring true. The 1920s had hummed with growth, expansion, and prosperity.

Consumer confidence had never seemed higher. Throughout the decade, great prosperity had become the watchword.

BOOM TIME FOR INDUSTRY AND INVESTORS

Economic progress seemed everywhere, as Americans emerged from the self-imposed rationing and sacrifice of World War I and went on a buying spree. Millions of people across the country bought their first everything—their first automobile, washing machine, camera, radio, refrigerator. These products came off America's assembly lines in an endless stream. As early as 1916 the number of cars produced annually in domestic plants topped 1 million. When the decade opened, in 1920, there were more than 8 million cars registered in the United States. By the end of the decade that number had mushroomed to 23 million. America's industrial output knew no bounds. More people were at work in U.S. factories and production plants than ever before, producing more goods than ever before. The U.S. economy was sometimes compared to an economic miracle.

Consumers in the United States were not the only ones to experience good times. U.S. investors had also had a field day. Overseas, U.S. investments nearly doubled from $3.98 billion in 1919 to $7.5 billion by 1929. The New York Stock Exchange, which served for many as the truest indicator of the nation's economic pulse, enjoyed phenomenal growth, especially after 1923. Stock purchases on the Exchange increased four-fold between 1923 and 1930. And stock sales were only outstripped by the rise in stock prices.

Americans had binged on stock investments during the 1920s. Altogether, investment in the stock market and in bonds rose sharper than any other economic indicator during the decade, faster, in fact, than the actual production or sales of manufactured goods.

Buying on Margin

It is no wonder. During the 1920s a would-be investor could make his or her stock purchases largely on credit. Under the rules in place for the New York Stock Exchange, investors could purchase stock through a practice called "buying on margin." It worked this way: An investor intent on purchasing $1,000 worth of stock at $10 per share could pay his broker (the person through whom the investor made his or her actual stock purchases) just one-tenth of the needed investment capital, or $100. The broker was all too happy to "loan" the investor the other $900, make the $1,000 investment, and wait for the profits to roll in.

With many stocks increasing in value during the 1920s at an average rate of 25 percent annually, that initial investment of $1,000 might have accrued to a value of $1,250 after being invested for a year. Then the investor might order his broker to sell his shares, pay the broker a fee of $100, and pocket the remaining $150, plus the initial investment of $1,000. Through this speculative system, everybody could win. The investor made money, the broker made money, the money invested in the market made someone money, and the economy continued to hum along. Year after year during America's "Roaring Twenties," the gambles paid off. Suddenly regular folks, not just the wealthy, were making money by playing the stock market and each investment seemed to represent a sure thing.

Soaring Stock Prices

Profits were there for the taking, it seemed. Certainly the New York Stock Exchange reflected this reality. In 1923 the market value of the Exchange's stock stood at $4 billion; it increased to $67 billion in just six years. It was not a flawless system, of course. There were losses on the market prior to 1929. Sometimes a given stock would tumble in value, the broker would have to call in his investment, causing the original investor to cash out short, and resulting in a loss. It was a gamble for the broker, as well. If a stock dropped, he might find himself overextended with "margin" loans to his investment clients, leaving him ruined.

Many were eager to ride the wave, however. Sometimes stock prices soared unbelievably. Take, for example, one company, Radio Corporation of America (RCA), part of an industry that was experiencing true growth at the time. In early 1928—the year of Hoover's election—RCA stock stood at $85 a share. By March 3 a share was worth $91.50. A week later, on March 10, it was worth $107 when the stock market opened, then closed that day at $120.50. Just two days later it had risen to $138.50. On March 13 it hit $160. By May it had reached the mile marker of $200. By November, with the election of Hoover over Democrat challenger Alfred Smith, RCA stock again doubled to $400, nearly five times its worth less than a year earlier. After a 70-point tumble in December, the stock recovered and began a slower rise, reaching $500 by mid-summer of 1929. At that point each share was split into five shares. Each was worth $101 by early September, and soon reached $114. Within just 18 months RCA stock had increased in value by a whopping 600 percent!

Only the most cautious investor could look at such increases and not be tempted to put money into stocks during the 1920s. The year 1928 presented additional stock miracles, including Chrysler, with a share of its stock increasing from $63 to $132—more than double. But the wave of investment was about to crest, and even collapse.

CORPORATE PROFITS

What was behind this drive in stock values during the 1920s? One answer is clear—corporate profits. Between 1916 and 1925 the profits gleaned by America's largest manufacturing companies amounted to an annual average of $730 million. That figure nearly doubled, to $1.4 billion, in the period from 1926 to the latter months of 1929! During 1929 alone corporate profits were actually three times what they had been in 1920. The stock prices simply reflected this ever-increasing level of corporate profit. Just as corporate profits tripled during the 1920s, so stock prices tripled during those same years.

Another reason why stock prices rose so significantly during the decade was that banks and brokerage companies were encouraging stock investment through their practice of "buying on margin." A typical stock purchase in the 1920s involved a broker or bank loan of half the stock's value. Such loans climbed from $1 billion in 1920 to $6 billion in 1928. Through this practice 1.5 million families became stock market investors, almost doubling the previous number and creating the largest number of investors to that point in U.S. history. Furthermore trading was constant and heavy, with 236 million shares traded in 1923, compared to 1.1 billion shares in 1928.

Finally, the stock market took on the appeal of a legitimate "get rich quick" scheme. Americans wanted to get in on the boom that the market seemed to represent. They listened to important movers-and-shakers in the corporate world, such as the director of General Motors and chairman of the Democratic Party, John J. Raskob. In 1928 he said the stock boom would continue for years, and that wealth was within the reach of nearly anyone who saved some money regularly to invest in the market. Writing an article for the *Ladies Home Journal* ("Everybody Ought to Be Rich"), Raskob stated, notes historian Dixon Wecter: "If a man saves fifteen dollars a week and invests in common stocks, at the end of twenty years he will have at least $80,000 and an income from investments of around $400 a month. He will be rich."

An unlucky Wall Street speculator, Walter Thornton of New York, offers to sell his car for way below its purchase price after the stock market crash of October 1929.

For hundreds of thousands of Americans, the formula for easy money and financial security was just too appealing to pass up.

THE STOCK MARKET CRASH

Reality caught up with the U.S. stock market in the autumn of 1929, when the giant bubble of speculation finally began to burst. In part, the timing was caused by Great Britain, where interest rates were raised to lure back investors who had abandoned British markets for the greener pastures of the U.S. stock market. Suddenly, foreign investors and an astute cadre of U.S. speculators saw the writing on the wall and began dumping their U.S. stocks.

The first significant shudder in the market was felt in September 1929, when stock prices fell without warning, only to recover as quickly as they had fallen. On October 21 another drop occurred. On October 23, a Wednesday, 6 million shares were sold, representing a withdrawal from the market of $4 billion in investment. Electric stock tickers were so pressed with information that traders across the country were reading numbers nearly two hours old.

Black Thursday, Black Tuesday

The next day, October 24, would be remembered as "Black Thursday," with orders to sell off stock spreading across the index. By noon nearly 13 million shares had been traded, setting a new record; the value of the market decreased by $9 billion. Stock tickers ran four hours behind. The day ended on an up tick, reducing the day's losses to approximately one-third of the previous day. Following the drop on Black Thursday the investment firm of J. P. Morgan and Company, with support from other large banks, hurriedly bought up as many stocks as they could just to restore public confidence in the market.

It was all for nothing. On October 29, 1929, a day recalled even today as "Black Tuesday," the market collapsed. That day 16 million shares were traded, and the industrial stock index dropped 43 points, destroying nearly all the gains made by the market during the previous 12 months. Multiple stocks lost almost all their value. For three weeks following "Black Tuesday," the market continued to free-fall. By the middle of November, the market had lost about one-third of its value, an amount representing $26 billion, or 40 percent of all stock that had existed on the Exchange just a month earlier.

Wall Street Suicides

The once powerful stockbrokers of New York were losing their silk shirts. Some, their livelihoods gone and their wealth evaporating, chose to end it all by leaping out of their office windows. One was the head of the Union Cigar Company, whose company's stock had dropped from $115 a share to $2. He took a dive from a ledge above the streets of New York City. Another jumper, this one in Milwaukee, left a suicide note that read, notes historian Robin Doak: "My body should go to science, my soul to Andrew W. Mellon [Hoover's Secretary of the Treasury], and sympathy to my creditors." A dark joke soon began to spread of hotel clerks questioning guests as they signed in for a room: "For sleeping or jumping?"

One of the most famous jumps was reported by Winston Churchill, who was to become Prime Minister of Great Britain in 1940. Churchill was staying at the Savoy-Plaza Hotel in New York the day after "Black Tuesday," and was awakened by a crowd on the street below. He wrote later: "Under my very window a gentleman cast himself down fifteen storeys and was dashed to pieces, causing a wild commotion and the arrival of the fire brigade."

Actually, Wall Street suicides became part of the myth of the Great Depression. New York City's chief medical officer reported on November 13, 1929, that just 44 suicides had taken place during the previous month, which included "Black Tuesday," a lower number than the 53 suicides reported during the same period a year earlier.

Crash Followed by Depression

Within another month, further stock slides represented a market loss of 50 percent of the value of stocks on the market back in September. And the decline continued over the next three years. The industrial index—a measure of performance of leading industrial shares—which was pegged at 452 in September 1929, hit bottom in July 1932 at 58.

But, when the stock market began to tumble off in late October 1929, it was not the cause of the long-term economic depression that followed. Instead, it was a symptom of the nation's less-than-healthy economy. In the first place, the vast majority of Americans were not invested in the market. Historians and economists estimate that just 3 million Americans—approximately 2.5 percent of the population— owned any stock at all. Thus, according to historian David M. Kennedy, "the Crash in itself had little direct or immediate economic effect on the typical American." The same would not be true, of course, of the Great Depression that was soon to engulf not just the United States, but most of the industrialized world.

CAUSES OF THE DEPRESSION

Several important circumstances, some of which were not within the scope of the U.S. government's control, were responsible for the Great Depression that spread across the United States and throughout the western industrialized nations after 1929.

A significant portion of the economic growth in the United States during the 1920s had been in two industries: construction and automobile sales. By the late 1920s both these industries were declining. Construction expenditures fell between 1926 and 1929, from $11 billion to $9 billion. Car sales were also down, dropping by one-third throughout 1929 until the Crash. Americans had now bought their Fords, Parkards, Studebakers, and Pierce-Arrows, and most were more than happy to hang on to them as long as pos-

SIGNS OF DISASTER

For many Americans, the stock market collapse in October 1929 was a shock. So many had considered the economy to be "bullet proof," experiencing a boom that might continue without end. But reality caught up with the nation that fateful fall. Yet, for some people, the collapse came as no surprise—a few Americans had seen it coming.

Some of them were in positions of power. One such was Smith Wildman Brookhart, a Republican senator from Iowa who was elected in 1920 and again in 1926. Brookhart was considered an "Insurgent Republican," because he was often critical of the economic politics of Republican presidents Harding and Coolidge. During a Senate hearing in 1928 Brookhart stated to "expert witness" Joseph Stagg Lawrence, a Princeton University economist, his opinion that the United States was "headed for the greatest panic in the history of the world," notes historian David A. Horowitz. Professor Lawrence dismissed Brookhart's claims as "the curious emissions of a provincial mind."

Among the others who spotted signs of coming disaster was a Minnesota senator, Henrik Shipstead, who noted before the Crash that 3,500 small banks had closed their doors across the country between 1920 and 1925. Herbert Hoover also saw it coming, and sold off most of his stock long before the bottom fell out of the market.

sible, ultimately cutting the nation's market for new automobiles. With drops in building and automobiles, dozens of "feeder" industries were impacted, including electronics, rubber, lumber, cement, and steel.

Poverty and Credit

A second cause of the Depression related to how good the "good times" of the 1920s had really been for the majority of Americans. It appears the economy was vibrant in many ways, but the wealth of the era was not evenly distributed to everyone. Even as late as 1929 more than 50 percent of U.S. families were living at or below the poverty line. This meant that they were too poor to buy the consumer goods that were, in part, fueling the economic boom. There were profits in major sectors of the economy, for farmers, industrial workers, and others, but the level of those profits did not generate enough income to create adequate markets. For example, between 1923 and 1929, manufacturing output per U.S. worker increased by 32 percent, yet during those same years real wages only increased by 8 percent. U.S. workers were more productive, but they were unable to afford the goods they were producing. Had manufacturers paid their workers better, those workers would have had greater purchasing power, which would have fed the economy.

Perhaps related to this is the third cause of the Depression—the level of the nation's credit structure. So many of those who were buying from the abundance of U.S. consumer goods being produced did so on credit. Unable to pay cash for the things they saw advertised, many were driven to make purchases on credit, through revolving credit plans, installment plans, and other newly created means. A family's parlor might feature a radio, vacuum sweeper, and nice furniture, but this did not mean they were able to afford such things. Farmers too were deeply in debt, with their lands mortgaged to the hilt, but with farm prices too low to allow them to pay off those debts. With so many small banks in small towns loaning farmers money, they became shaky institutions, as their customers were sometimes unable to pay or simply defaulted on their loans. In addition, some of the larger U.S. banks were incautiously investing in the stock market or otherwise giving out their own bad loans.

The International Situation

The fourth and fifth causes of the Great Depression in America were related more directly to the country's international economic situation. While U.S. companies had produced an abundance of goods during World War I, when European powers needed everything from tents to trucks, the demand for U.S. goods fell off dramatically after the war. Postwar Europeans rebuilt their own industries and reclaimed their farm fields, so they did not need to rely on U.S. goods and food. Tariffs were commonplace among the industrialized nations of the West, which limited trade between them. Some tariff rates were as high as they had ever been, keeping U.S. goods out of foreign markets and limiting the sale of U.S. products.

Lastly, an important factor leading to the Depression was the international debt structure. During the war European nations had borrowed billions from the U.S. Treasury to help pay for their war effort. Those Allied nations, particularly Britain and France, had intended to repay their own debts by extracting reparations, or war damages, from the defeated Central Powers, especially Germany. But Germany and Austria emerged from the war with their economies in shambles, and their governments unable to pay. If the war's losers could not pay the war's winners, U.S. bankers were left holding the bag. In addition, U.S. banking houses loaned Germany a further $1.2 billion between 1924 and 1930, in an effort to help the country recover from the war and become a viable trading partner for the future.

Rich and Poor

All this meant that the booming prosperity of America's "Roaring Twenties" had represented a warped or lopsided economy. The production of consumer goods was always running ahead of the average person's ability to buy them. In fact, the U.S. economy of the 1920s represented an extremely uneven distribution of wealth. In 1929 the top 0.1 percent of U.S. households had a combined income equal to that of the bottom 42 percent of U.S. households, who numbered 11.5 million families. That same 0.1 percent of wealthy Americans also owned one out of every three dollars held as savings. Approximately 80 percent of families in the United States had no money saved at all. Similarly, 71 percent of U.S. families had annual incomes of $2,500 or less (equivalent to about $32,000 today).

The U.S. economy of the 1920s had appeared, if one did not look behind the stage set, booming, progressive, and pointing endlessly upward. But by 1929 the bubble had burst, and the nation found itself engulfed in the deepest economic collapse in its history. Yet 1929 was only the beginning. Over the next four years, the nation's economy continued to slide downward into a hole that seemed to have no bottom.

2
Hoover's Depression

When the Great Depression finally hit, it hit hard and quickly. Following the collapse of the stock market, every other loose end in the economy unraveled. It was difficult, at first, for many in America to understand what was happening. Wall Street may have imploded, but they could still see the nation's factories, mines, and foundries ready to maintain production. They could see millions of farms, the land still intact, ready to produce their annual harvest. But, with the crush of each passing month, many parts of the great U.S. economic machine either slowed down or ground to a complete standstill.

BANKS BEGIN TO FAIL

Everything was connected. The collapse of the market deterred many potential investors from investing. Those who had loaned money called in those loans, desperate for cash. Money seemed in short supply. Storekeepers and small business owners sold less, as factories produced less or closed their doors and padlocked their gates. Farmers lost markets for their produce, causing them to make less profit, and making them fall behind on their mortgage payments. Banks, also in fervent need of cash, called in farm mortgages, house mortgages, and auto loans, leaving some of their clients homeless, farmless, stranded. Millions of Americans lined up at countless teller windows demanding to withdraw their hard-earned savings.

But soon enough the money was gone. It actually was never all there to begin with. While a depositor's savings passbook might state that he or she had $50, $100, or $500 in that bank, the bank could not produce all its deposits at once, for so much of that money had been invested or loaned out. With so many people demanding to withdraw their savings, the banks could only admit that the money was held symbolically in this house loan and that farm mortgage, but was not actually sitting in the bank's vault. Quickly, banks began to fail.

With banks going out of business, those who tried to remain in business found it difficult to secure future loans. Builders had to stop construction, for example, because they could not get enough working capital to continue.

THE NEW JOBLESS

The nation's institutions—banks, businesses, farms, all of it—became shaky. Almost nothing remained reliable. At the bottom of all this chaotic economic mess was America's working class, the millions of ordinary people who had always worked, always paid their bills, and tried to make their way in the world. Suddenly, they were without jobs, receiving notices at their places of employment telling them they did not need to come to work anymore, that their jobs were gone, the store was closing, the factory was shutting

PANIC AS THE BANKS START TO FAIL

During the Depression, banks suffered not only from failing investments as share prices fell but also from loss of income from people who had taken out loans but could not pay them back. When the stock market crashed, savers ran to the banks to get their money. By the winter of 1932–33 some 5,000 banks had run out of money and closed.

A crowd of people gathers outside a bank that is struggling to survive. Some people are seeking to withdraw their savings. Others are there to witness the chaos and pandemonium in the financial world.

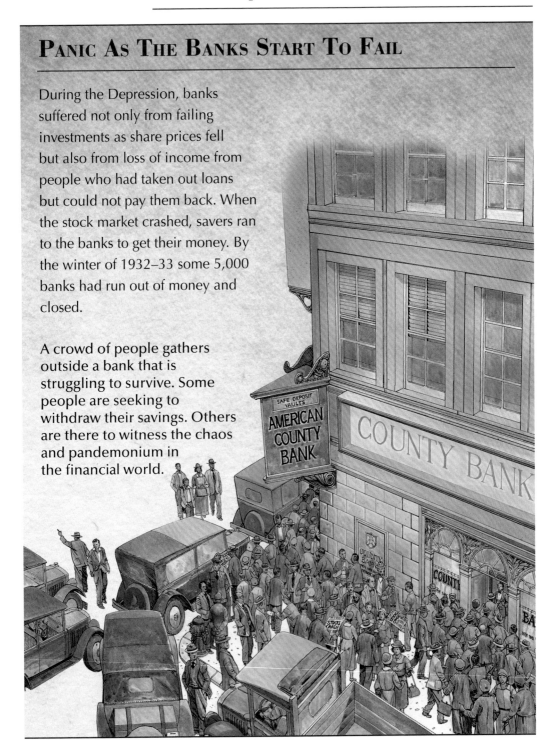

down. Without work, they could not buy anything. If they could not buy, others who still had jobs had fewer customers to make things for, which put their jobs at risk as well. The consequential effect caused unemployment to spread rapidly and widely like a plague.

The new jobless were not the old-line poor who had always struggled at the bottom of the economic ladder. Many of the newly unemployed had always been solid citizens, middle-class workers such as bank tellers, factory men, female telephone operators, garage mechanics, and office clerks—those who had represented the backbone of the U.S. economy for decades. They lost their jobs, farmers lost their farms, and the great instruments of prosperity stopped playing. Many in the rural areas left for the cities, where they thought they could find work, or simply packed up everything they had left after losing their farms and headed down the road in search of work. Larger numbers of Americans than ever in the nation's history were living in poverty. Families became desperate for just the necessities.

In 1939 American writer John Steinbeck described these desperate circumstances on the pages of his most famous novel, *The Grapes of Wrath*. He drew a hard picture of those who piled their families in a Ford Model-T and lit out in search of work:

> And then the dispossessed were drawn west—from Kansas, Oklahoma, Texas, New Mexico; from Nevada and Arkansas families, tribes, dusted out, tractored out. Carloads, caravans, homeless and hungry; twenty thousand and fifty thousand and a hundred thousand and two hundred thousand. They streamed over the mountains, hungry and restless—restless as ants, scurrying to find work to do—to lift, to push, to pull, to pick, to cut—anything, any burden to bear, for food.

HOOVER RESPONDS

When Herbert Hoover was inaugurated on March 4, 1929, as the nation's third conservative Republican president in a row, the vast majority of the Americans could not have been happier. His message to a crowd of 50,000 gathered on that rainy day in Washington, as well as to a larger radio audience, was prophetic: "We are steadily building a new race—a new civilization great in its own attainments... Ours is a land rich in resources; stimulating in its glorious beauty; filled with millions of happy homes... No country is more loved by its people... I have no fears for the future of the country. It is bright with hope."

When the Crash came in the fall of 1929 and the country began to slide into an economic morass, Hoover, who had only been in office for eight months prior to "Black Tuesday," remained, at least publicly, optimistic. He had believed for several years that the stock market had been in need of a serious adjustment, a return to reality. He insisted that, despite such downturns, the U.S. economy was fundamentally sound. Depressions had happened before in the nation's history—in 1807, 1819, 1837, 1857, 1873, and 1893—and this depression would not last forever. Hoover used the word "depression" to describe the economic downturn, rather than the previously used terms "panic" or "crisis" to try to steer people away from panicking. Recovery would take place, Hoover assured, possibly even arriving sooner than circumstances would indicate. In the meantime, he took several overt steps to utilize the power of the federal government in fighting the Depression.

Despite the traditional view that President Hoover did nothing to meet the challenges of the Depression, he began making moves within days or weeks of the stock market crash. He summoned the heads of major U.S. corporations to the White House, calling on them to cooperate with the government by maintaining, as much as possible, a continued level of production, employment, wages, and limited labor conflicts. He threw together a raft of emergency federal agencies and bureaus to focus on the primary problem of increasing unemployment and the need for direct relief. Hoover also supported large-scale construction projects for city and state government buildings and other public works, requesting $150 million from Congress to build new government facilities. But these steps only had a marginal impact on the nation's declining economy.

Thousands of unemployed migrants lived in this shantytown in Seattle in the early 1930s. They earned a few cents each day sorting bottles and cans. Such towns became known as "Hoovervilles."

In addition, Hoover took steps that only made the depression worse. He signed off on a new tariff bill, the Smoot-Hawley Tariff of 1930, which raised import duties on farm imports by 70 percent and on industrial goods by 40 percent, all of which only hurt America's place in international trade. Then the Federal Reserve Board threw an additional monkey wrench in the gears of recovery by raising interest rates in 1931. One result was a decline in the amount of money in circulation. In 1930–31 the nation's money supply dropped by one-third, and the results were catastrophic.

Industrialists, promises to Hoover aside, began cutting back on production and reducing their number of workers, fearing a drop in consumer demand. Beyond that, times were so bad and looking worse that many investors simply began pulling their money out of the U.S. marketplace. Hoover saw what was happening and unrealistically called for those with money and resources to stick their necks out a little further in support of the U.S. economy. Historian Robin Santos Doak recalls the words of the president in February 1931: "We are going through a period when character and courage are on trial; where the very faith that is within us is under test."

A DEEPENING PROBLEM

America's depression was also worsened by Europe's economic collapse. In the spring of 1931 France, desperate for money, called for payment of loans that had been taken out by Germany and Austria, resulting in the collapse of Austria's largest bank. In the aftermath investors pulled their gold deposits from other German and Austrian banks, which forced France and Britain, along with other European nations, to abandon the gold standard. This led European investors to sell off their U.S. assets, while asking for gold in return. The result was a vast sell off of investment in the New York Stock Exchange and U.S. money markets, which ultimately led to the failure of 2,000 U.S. banks during the last six months of 1931. Tied to these trends, employment in the United States dropped by 12 percent, and wages for those who still had jobs fell by 30 percent.

Many of these international circumstances were not under President Hoover's control. But, since they led to a worsening of the U.S. economy, he began taking greater steps to involve the power of the federal government in addressing the issues of the Depression. It should be said that Hoover was not at this stage considered by the American people to be the one responsible for the bad economy. He had said publicly that the Depression would run a natural course and eventually end. Most Democrats, in 1930, agreed. Even when the 1930 elections were held in November, the Democrats managed to win control of the House, although the Senate remained in Republican hands. At this stage few Americans were blaming Hoover or his party for the downturn in the nation's economy.

Nevertheless, things continued to get worse. For U.S. banks, times were crushing. In 1929 more than 600 U.S. banks closed their doors. The following year more than 1,000 more joined them. In 1931 a further 2,000 U.S. banks went out of business. For U.S. farmers, there seemed to be no end to their decline. In 1929 a bushel of wheat had sold for $1.03, but the price had dropped to just 36 cents by 1931. Unemployment was rising, although no one knew exactly how many Americans were without jobs because at that time the federal government did not keep such records accurately. Some experts put the number of unemployed at around 15 million. But that was only half the story. For many of those who still had jobs, they were receiving less pay. Many were only partially employed, leaving them "under-employed." By 1932 the average industrial wage in America had slipped to just 50 percent of what it had been in 1928.

A contemporary cartoon during the presidential campaign of 1932 shows an unemployed man contemplating President Hoover's optimistic assessment of the state of the country.

No Federal Welfare

None of this was to Hoover's liking, of course. But as he faced this mountain of economic bad news, he became gloomy and perhaps even confused. He tried to project a publicly optimistic image as the nation's leader. As late as 1932, he said to a group of businessmen: "Prosperity is just around the corner." Privately, though, he struggled.

Hoover was a humane individual, someone who did not like to see people suffer. He had seen plenty of that during World War I when he served, without pay, as the director of the U.S. food relief program that fed millions of starving Europeans. But he was convinced that the government should remain largely detached from the economy and not interfere in the natural tendencies of a capitalist state. Free enterprise, he continued to feel, would eventually bring the country back from the brink of economic ruin.

Just as importantly, Hoover believed the federal government should not engage in direct relief by providing monies or other support to the poor, starving, or unemployed. For him, it was a moral issue. He said: "It is not the function of the government to relieve individuals of their responsibilities to their neighbors, or to relieve private institutions of their responsibilities to the public." Direct federal welfare, he said, would weaken or ruin the moral fiber of the U.S. people.

RETHINKING THE GOVERNMENT'S ROLE

Something had to be done, however. In 1931 Hoover took additional, overt steps to fight the Depression, becoming the first U.S. president to commit significant federal power and resources to meet the challenge of an economic disaster. He requested $2.25 billion from Congress to be used for public works projects, representing the costliest federal program to that point in U.S. history. One of the approved projects was a huge dam to be built on the Colorado River, which would one day be called the Hoover Dam.

Finance for Reconstruction

Hoover also signed off on a bill creating, in early 1932, a new federal agency called the Reconstruction Finance Corporation (RFC), the first such national agency ever set up to do battle with an economic depression. Originally capitalized at $500 million, this agency was authorized to lend up to $2 billion to struggling private institutions, including banks, insurance firms, farm mortgage companies, and railroads. The loans to banks would be especially important, since they would be able to then loan money to other businesses. The idea was that this money would trickle down, to get production and sales moving again and to provide funds for new building projects. All this economic stimulus would create new jobs and allow others to keep their jobs longer. Money would return to the streets, people would spend it, and the entire economic cycle would be complete, allowing the economy to begin to hum once more.

A few months later, Congress passed the Emergency and Relief Construction Act, which extended the RFC's power to lend, this time up to $1.5 billion to local and state governments for public works projects. The agency was also authorized to loan an additional $300 million to help the states provide direct relief to their citizens.

Yet all these hundreds of millions of dollars pumped into the economy through the auspices of the RFC—$1.2 billion within the first six months of its existence—did not actually trickle down adequately or stimulate the economy dramatically. Only 10 percent of state-level direct relief was doled out immediately. Part of the problem was Hoover's unwavering economic philosophy—that the economy would not readjust properly without a higher level of investor morale.

That, the president insisted, depended on the federal government maintaining a balanced budget and showing fiscal restraint. To cover the cost of such programs as the RFC, Hoover insisted on raising taxes. That move only managed, notes historian David Horowitz, to "deplete investment capital and purchasing power." While Hoover's steps toward government intervention on behalf of the U.S. economy were bolder than any taken by any previous president, he hamstrung his own programs and worked against their true potential.

However, such moves as creating the RFC would lay the groundwork for the rebuilding efforts of the Roosevelt administration that would follow Hoover's presidency. Historian Amity Shlaes recalls the words of Rexford Guy Tugwell, a former economics professor, who became FDR's Under Secretary of Agriculture and a key New Deal architect: "I once made a list of New Deal ventures begun during Hoover's years as secretary of commerce and then as president… The New Deal owed much to what he had begun."

A CONTINUING SLIDE

For three years Americans by the millions had tried to cope with the Depression, but circumstances continued to worsen. Forty million people had descended into poverty. In some U.S. cities, such as Akron, Ohio, unemployment stood between 60 and 80 percent. An estimated 1 million citizens—including 200,000 children—were homeless, riding the roads, riding the rails, living in migrant camps, a world of drifters later described by Steinbeck in *The Grapes of Wrath:*

> *And a homeless hungry man… drove his old car into a town. He scoured the farms for work. Where can we sleep the night?*

Well, there's a Hooverville on the edge of the river. There's a whole raft of Okies there.

He drove his old car to Hooverville. He never asked again, for there was a Hooverville on the edge of every town.

The rag town lay close to water; and the houses were tents, and weed-thatched, paper houses, a great junk pile. The man drove his family in and became a citizen of Hooverville—always they were called Hooverville. The man put up his own tent as near to water as he could get; or if he had no

PUTTING THE DEPRESSION TO MUSIC

The Great Depression delivered hardships to millions of Americans, especially those working-class folks who saw themselves as victims of an economy that had imploded on them through no fault of their own. One talented musician who put a voice to much of that frustration was an American folk singer from Oklahoma, whom some referred to as a "Shakespeare in Overalls"—Woody Guthrie.

Guthrie was a teenager when the Depression hit in the late 1920s. Born in the Midwest in 1912 and named after President Woodrow Wilson, who became the Democratic Party nominee just a week before he was born, Guthrie grew up in rural Oklahoma and the Texas Panhandle.

His father was a part-time cowboy who taught his young son a host of western songs. But Woody's early years were filled with misery: His sister died after setting herself on fire; his father went broke and turned to alcohol; and his mother descended into insanity.

At an early age Guthrie was on his own, drifting across the country, playing the guitar and harmonica. He had a natural affinity for the underclass of working Americans and wrote songs addressing the difficulties of the people he met riding in railway boxcars and sharing meals in migrant camps. He played his music anywhere he could, including such commonplace venues as carnivals, rodeos, and county fairs.

tent, he went to the city dump and brought back cartons and built a house of corrugated paper. And when the rains came the house melted and washed away. He settled in Hooverville and he scoured the countryside for work, and the little money he had went for gasoline to look for work.

Everywhere the misery spread. Between 1929 and 1932 an average of 100,000 workers lost their jobs each week. A writer for *The Atlantic* magazine described the prevailing

Although privately Guthrie became so angry with the nation's leaders that he talked of robbing banks, he wrote folk ballads instead. He wrote about the difficulties brought on by hard times, the Dust Bowl, and the perils of workers trying to organize labor unions. In time he became radicalized, a favorite of Socialist and Communist groups across the country; a performer who brought an angry soul of protest to so many of his folk tunes. He wrote hundreds of songs, including "This Train Is Bound for Glory," "Chain Around My Leg," "Going Down the Road Feeling Bad," "Hard Ain't It Hard," and "Dust Bowl Blues." In his "Dust Can't Kill Me," Woody spoke for many Midwesterners who had experienced the silt-laden winds of the Great Plains:

That old dust storm killed my baby,
But it won't kill me, lord.
No, it won't kill me.

Woody Guthrie's signature song would be his ballad, "God Blessed America," which is remembered today by most people as "This Land is Your Land." Its lyrics ring with poetic allusions, including "endless skyways," "golden valleys," "diamond deserts," and "wheat fields waving." Despite his hard-bitten distain for those who victimized the underdog, Woody Guthrie never lost his love for America. Throughout the Depression and until his death in 1967, he never lost faith in his country and remained a consistent voice on behalf of the nation's underclass. And he provided inspiration for many new folk musicians, including Bob Dylan.

national response to the Depression. Fear, he wrote, was "the dominant emotion of contemporary America—fear of losing one's job, fear of reduced salary or wages, fear of eventual destitution and want."

The strain placed on local and state governments to respond to those without work, or homeless, or hungry was immense and their responses inadequate. The RFC sent monies to the states to provide direct relief, but it was never enough. The state of Pennsylvania, for example, was only able to borrow enough from the agency to provide the equivalent of 3 cents a day to its unemployed workers. Hoover's Federal Farm Board worked to help out farmers by buying up surplus supplies of wheat and cotton. But when the agency began experiencing major losses, it abandoned the program. As farm incomes dropped by 50 percent in 1932, the farm board found itself a half billion dollars in the red.

Hoover did take other steps, such as establishing the Federal Home Loan Bank Act of 1932, which created a home mortgage board that divided the country up into 12 districts and handed out $125 million to provide loans to struggling banks and mortgage companies. But everything kept falling apart. The economy continued to slide until millions of Americans, who had given Hoover the benefit of the doubt earlier, now decided that he was at least partially responsible for the Depression. The President's name became a joke, applied to circumstances that mocked him. Homeless families lived in shanty communities called "Hoovervilles." Newspapers used by vagrants to cover themselves at night to stay warm were called "Hoover blankets." A "Hoover Flag" was an empty pants pocket turned inside out.

THE NATION VOTES

Against the backdrop of this negative national mood, Americans looked ahead to the presidential election of 1932. Dur-

ing the summer the World War I veterans known as the
Bonus Marchers had come out in force in Washington in
support of legislation to pay them their bonus early, rather
than at the scheduled date of 1945. Their hopes were dashed
by a Senate vote against the bonus, followed by U.S. Army
troops who drove them out of the nation's capital. The state
of affairs in the country was ugly, and many people were
desperate.

Roosevelt is Selected

The Democrats met in convention, optimistic of their
chances of regaining the White House for the first time in
12 years. Eyeing victory in November, delegates at the convention chose New York Governor Franklin Delano Roosevelt (sometimes known as FDR), a distant cousin of former
president Theodore Roosevelt. Roosevelt was from an old
Dutch family, a member of the wealthy, patrician class who
had attended Harvard, and studied law at Columbia. He had
served during Wilson's administration as assistant secretary
of the navy, the same job his cousin Theodore had held when
the Spanish–American War broke out in 1898.

Roosevelt had been on the Democratic national ticket
before, having run as the party's vice presidential candidate
in 1920. The next year he had been struck down by an attack
of poliomyelitis (polio), which paralyzed him and left him
unable to walk unaided for the rest of his life. But Roosevelt
had persevered and been elected as governor of New York
for two terms, in 1928 and 1930. In the tradition of his progressive cousin, FDR had supported unemployment relief,
banking reform, farm aid, conservation, and an expansion
of his state's capacity to produce hydroelectric power. He
received the Democratic nomination on the third ballot.

Roosevelt's rhetoric had helped him gain his party's confidence. He had delivered a radio address on April 7, 1932,

a coast-to-coast broadcast out of Albany facilitated by the National Broadcasting Company (NBC) and sponsored by Lucky Strike cigarettes, in which he said he was campaigning for the "forgotten man at the bottom of the economic pyramid." When his nomination was secured, Roosevelt broke precedence and flew to the convention to accept it in person. There he told the assembled Democratic Party delegates, "I pledge you, I pledge myself, to a new deal for the American people." He promised to lower tariffs and provide adequate relief for those out of work. He said he would go to Washington as president and summon a "brain trust" of experts to help him formulate his economic strategy, including university professors, economists, and social planners. Following FDR's speech the delegates cheered wildly, while a band played a song that had been written in 1929—the year of the Crash—for a Metro-Goldwyn-Mayer (MGM) movie, *Chasing Rainbows*. It was a tune destined to become the Democrats' theme through election day:

> *Happy days are here again!*
> *The skies above are clear again!*
> *Let's all sing a song of cheer again—*
> *Happy days are here again!*

A Campaign of Optimism

Throughout the campaign Roosevelt rode a tidal wave of support. Hoover spoke out against FDR's promises, saying that lower tariffs would only guarantee that "the grass will grow in the streets of a hundred cities" and that "weeds will overrun the fields of a million farms." For some listeners, Hoover seemed to be talking about the present rather than the future. As FDR campaigned, he appeared optimistic—a cheerful individual who exuded confidence. His physical disability never entered the campaign, because the press never reported that Roosevelt could not move about without leg braces or canes. Today only two photographs exist of FDR in a wheelchair. Both were taken at one of the Roosevelt homes, on the same day and by the same photographer, a female friend of the family.

For three years Americans had listened to Hoover's encouragements about the economy, but they no longer believed in him. The result was a smashing victory for FDR, his vice presidential running mate, Texan John Nance Garner, and the Democrats. Roosevelt won with nearly 23 million votes over Hoover's 15.7 million (the electoral vote was lopsided at 472 to 59), representing victories in all but six states. In addition, the Democrats won control of both houses of Congress.

"THE ONLY THING WE HAVE TO FEAR"

Between Roosevelt's election and his inauguration on March 4, 1933, President Hoover approached him about working together on programs to address the worsening economy. Roosevelt refused, telling Hoover that such steps would only limit his decisions prematurely before he even entered office. In the meantime, the nation's banking system was falling apart.

In February Roosevelt was targeted by an assassin named Giuseppe Zangara. The would-be assassin missed, but instead accidentally shot the mayor of Chicago, Anton Cermak, while he was shaking hands with the president-elect in Miami. Before being taken to a local hospital Cermak said to Roosevelt, "I'm glad it was me instead of you." He died later of his wounds.

On Inauguration Day Roosevelt first attended a brief service at Washington's St. John's Episcopal Church, then stopped by the Mayflower Hotel to meet with advisors about the looming banking crisis. Then he rode with a glum-faced

Hoover down Pennsylvania Avenue to the inauguration platform on the east side of the Capitol, where machine gun nests had been placed on the roof for security. With the support of his son, FDR walked to the podium and recited the entire oath of office by heart, instead of simply saying "I do" as had been the custom.

Then before thousands of gathered citizens, radio microphones, and newsreel crews, spread out before him on 10 acres (4 hectares) of spring grass, and with countless millions listening to him on radios across the country, Franklin Delano Roosevelt assured the people of the United States, with words that, for many Americans, still ring true today:

> *"This is preeminently the time to speak the truth, the whole truth, frankly and boldly. Nor need we shrink from honestly facing conditions in our country today. This great Nation will endure as it has endured, will revive and will prosper. So, first of all, let me assert my firm belief that the only thing we have to fear is fear itself."*

3
Launching the New Deal

The new president wasted no time. FDR skipped the usual inaugural ball and went straight to work on the evening of March 4, 1933, the lights burning in the White House long after dark. There were many problems to address. That spring approximately 25 percent of the U.S. workforce was without jobs. Wages had dropped from a high in 1929 of $53 billion down to $31 billion. Farm incomes had dropped in those same years from $12 billion to $5 billion. While farmers were barely hanging on, given the low commodity prices, millions of Americans living in urban centers could not afford the cost of groceries, with butter at 39 cents a pound, prime rib roast at 21 cents, and a dozen eggs at 19 cents.

Industrial production was half what it had been less than four years earlier. The labor movement was collapsing, with only 6 percent of the workforce unionized. Annual car sales had fallen from 4.5 million to just over 1 million. The construction sector had fallen from $8.7 billion in 1929 to $1.4 billion in 1933. "Catastrophe" was the word everyone used to describe an economy that refused to hit bottom. And looming large on the economic horizon was the banking crisis. With thousands of banks having already closed, Americans were desperate to withdraw their deposits, causing "runs" on the banks. Already, governors in 29 states had declared banking moratoriums and put limits on the amount a person might withdraw.

A LEGISLATIVE STORM

What soon emerged from FDR's leadership was a flurry of legislation sent from the White House to Capitol Hill. All of it was designed to battle the Depression by arming the federal government with programs and agencies, each intended to target a particular problem. Roosevelt had spoken during the campaign of creating a "New Deal" for the American people. In 1932 he did not have a clear concept of exactly what that New Deal would include. But that spring he began to put some meat on the bone. His was largely an experimental approach. He said of his proposed programs: "It is common sense to take a method and try it. If it fails, admit it frankly and try another." Early in FDR's presidency a friend commented to the president that, if his answers to the Depression succeeded, he would go down as the greatest president ever; however, if the programs failed, his would be a presidency reviled by Americans everywhere. Historian Allen Weinstein recalls FDR's response: "If I fail, I shall be the last."

Ultimately, Roosevelt's New Deal was less a carefully thought out set of studied answers, and more a jumble of creative, improvised programs, thrown together as quickly as possible, and backed with executive orders or as approved legislation that passed quickly through Congress. Through his first two terms as president FDR's economic packages came in three stages, the first hammered out during his first "Hundred Days" in office in 1933. Stage two followed in 1935, and his last set of steps to address the Depression arrived in 1938.

Teamwork and Persuasion

Little connected one part of the New Deal's programs to another. Perhaps the unifying link was Roosevelt himself, especially his personality. He was not the New Deal's creator, really, for he was not a man of ideas or of great solutions, but one of action. He surrounded himself with his "Brain Trust," those professional and academic advisors who brought ideas and plans to him, and he transformed those proposals he approved of into reality, with the help of Congress. Generally, Roosevelt pursued moderate reform, never intending to "throw the baby out with the bath water" by abandoning capitalism or democracy, as other nations did during those same years.

Fortunately, Franklin Roosevelt's greatest asset was his capacity to persuade others. He was blessed, of course, at the opening of his presidency with Democrat majorities in both houses and a Republican opposition less interested in opposing and more in cooperating. During the initial stages of creating his New Deal programs, non-partisanship was the order of the day. One representative, notes historian James Kirby Martin, admitted: "I had as soon start a mutiny in the face of a foreign foe as… [go] against the program of the President." Republicans were ready that spring of 1933 to give Roosevelt almost unlimited power to address the challenges of the Depression. Popular cowboy humorist Will Rogers even joked of FDR: "If he burned down the Capitol we would cheer and say, 'Well, at least he got a fire started anyhow.'"

SALVAGING THE NATION'S BANKS

One of FDR's first targets was the banking crisis. Ten million people had lost a significant proportion of their savings through thousands of bank failures. On Sunday, March 5, just 24 hours after taking the oath of office, Roosevelt ordered a four-day bank holiday, which ended all bank transactions. Then, on March 9, he sent legislation to the new Congress, which had opened its first session only the previous day, in the form of the Emergency Banking Relief Bill. This was partially based on conservative reforms, proposed earlier by the Hoover administration, which allowed the RFC to buy stock in shaky banks and keep them solvent until they reorganized. The bill reached Capitol Hill around 1 P.M. An act had passed by 8:36 P.M. Due to a weekend the banks did not reopen until Monday, March 13, and they did so with the backing of the federal government. Deposits and gold began to flow back into the banking system.

Meanwhile Roosevelt went on the radio on March 12 to deliver the first of the national messages that would be known as his "Fireside Chats," to assure the American people that the banks were solvent. The government had even chartered planes to deliver stacks of newly printed money to banks across the country, to make certain there was enough money available when they reopened. Confidence returned. Soon deposits were outstripping withdrawals. In the words of one of FDR's New Deal "Brain Trust" team, Columbia professor Raymond Moley: "Capitalism was saved in eight days."

His deft handling of the banking crisis made FDR a national hero during his first two weeks in office. During his first week alone the White House received nearly a half million letters from grateful Americans. Under Hoover, the White House mailroom had operated with one person. Suddenly, 70 letter handlers were needed to process the crushing volume of mail praising FDR.

To further help the nation's banking system, three months later Congress passed the Glass-Steagall Banking Act of 1933. This act gave the Federal Reserve greater control over banks by monitoring their lending practices. It also created the Federal Deposit Insurance Corporation (FDIC), which

President Franklin Delano Roosevelt gives one of his "Fireside Chats." During the Depression he regularly used radio broadcasts to alleviate Americans' anxiety and explain how he would improve things.

provided government backing for deposits. Bank runs by uncertain depositors had left the banking system in chaos. On the day FDR was inaugurated the nation's 5,500 banks had only $6 billion in cash to cover $41 billion in deposits. The new FDIC guaranteed deposits up to a specific amount per bank. Initially, the amount was set at $2,500, but it was raised to $5,000 the following year. Over the years, the amount was further raised to $10,000 in 1950, $15,000 in 1966, $20,000 in 1969, and to $100,000 in 2008. (During the financial crisis in the spring of 2009, the limit was raised temporarily to $250,000.)

FIFTEEN MAJOR BILLS

But banking reform, while important, was only the beginning of the legislation passed during Roosevelt's first Hundred Days. All told, 15 major pieces of legislation were rammed through Congress from spring to early summer, with FDR targeting a gallery of economic woes in a scattergun approach. There were direct relief programs, such as the Federal Emergency Relief Act. There were farm bills, banking laws, and an act to bolster the railroad industry. At first Roosevelt was opposed to deficit spending and was just as interested as Hoover had been in maintaining a balanced budget. Much of the early legislation of those months, such as cutting federal spending and an excise tax on beer, was conservative—even Hoover could have supported it.

One of Roosevelt's key goals was to establish a "managed currency." Gold was, to the president and others, a questionable benchmark for determining money's value. People were starting to hoard gold as a security blanket against a drop in the value of the nation's currency. To protect the nation's gold reserves and prevent hoarding, Roosevelt issued an order for all private holders of gold to surrender their holdings for paper currency, then he removed the country from the gold standard. It was FDR's hope that altering the nation's money supply, by emphasizing paper currency and no longer pegging gold to dollars, would create inflation. Normally rises in prices have a negative connotation, but the president and his advisors believed that higher prices would give relief to those in debt and serve as an incentive to industry to increase production.

To achieve the desired inflation, Roosevelt ordered the Treasury Department to purchase gold, even as the price continued to steadily rise. This helped raise gold's value from $21 an ounce in 1933 to $35 an ounce by the following year. Gold maintained that value over the next 40 years! While the policy did increase the amount of dollars in circulation (some earlier critics of the economy had claimed that money was in too short supply), the inflation it caused angered "sound-money" supporters. In early 1934, FDR placed the United States back on a limited gold standard to encourage international trade. Until 1971 the U.S. government paid its foreign bills, when asked, in gold at the rate of $35 an ounce. Nevertheless domestic circulation of gold connected to the money supply remained illegal, making gold coins little more than collector's items, not legal tender.

A BOOST FOR YOUNG WORKERS

The Great Depression had thrown more Americans out of work than any previous economic crisis in U.S. history. While the sinking economy did not hit every group of workers equally, it struck hard against young workers, whose labor was needed more than ever to help support their families. To provide work for young men, Roosevelt gave his support to establishing a labor program, called the Civilian Conservation Corps (CCC). It was created by the Reforestation Relief Act, passed on March 31, 1933—one of the most unique pieces of legislation passed during the Hundred Days. At its

A recruitment poster for the Civilian Conservation Corps (CCC) produced by the Works Progress Administration (WPA), which was set up in 1935.

heart, the CCC was a wonderful idea: Supply jobs for young males in national and state parks. It proved to be one of the New Deal's most popular programs.

The first enlistee to sign up was a 19-year-old New Yorker, Fiore Rizzo, who walked into a recruiting station in Manhattan, notes historian Adam Cohen, "and declared he wanted to work in the woods." Roosevelt advisor, Henry Wallace (who would serve as FDR's second vice president after the 1940 election), spoke on the radio and explained what the CCC was: "This is primarily a relief program… [T]he men who enroll are not seeking charity; they want an opportunity to make their way."

Saving for their Families and Future

By mid-summer of 1933 the CCC, administered by America's peacetime army and the U.S. Forest Service, had hired 275,000 youngsters between the ages of 18 and 25 to leave their homes and work outdoors on a host of conservation projects in 1,300 camps. This represented a greater number of men than had signed up for service in the Spanish–American War just over a generation earlier. Eventually nearly 3 million young men worked for the CCC, including 200,000 blacks and 40,000 Indians. The work they did was of immediate importance, with longstanding results.

The CCC boys signed on for six months of service with the option to "re-enlist" for a total of two years. They were paid $30 a month and the CCC sent the lion's share (typically $25) back home to support their family. Often the boys put the left-over $5 on an account in their camp's canteen, where they could buy soda, candy bars, toiletries, and writing stationery to let their family back home know how they were doing. They needed little money for themselves. In many ways, life in the CCC mirrored the military. The boys lived in barracks, which they often built themselves. They ate in mess halls similar to those found on army bases. They were provided with clothing, although this was not a uniform. They took orders from army officers.

Few groups of workers in America labored as hard as the CCC boys. During the program's tenure, between 1933 and 1943, the CCC planted 1.5 billion trees and constructed 140,000 miles (225,000 kilometers) of roads and trails in countless parks around the country. They built rustic lodges, bridges, fire towers, campgrounds, and museums. They opened up caves for tourists by pouring concrete steps and

THE BONUS MARCH OF 1933

During Roosevelt's Hundred Days the Bonus Marchers returned to Washington. Having been driven out of Anacostia Flats the previous summer, thousands of veterans of the Great War were now ready to seek their bonus from another president. By May 3,000 of them were in Washington.

Roosevelt, who had stated during his campaign that Hoover's treatment of the Bonus Marchers had doomed his reelection, did not intend to make the same mistakes. He ordered the army to help set up an encampment for them outside the capital, at the site of an abandoned fort across the Potomac in Virginia. Tents were erected, along with latrines, showers,

and fully equipped mess halls, where the vets received three meals every day, free of charge. FDR issued an executive order to provide funds for the entire setup.

The Marchers still wanted their bonus, and they invited the president to come out and visit with them about it. He declined, stating: "You know, I have been working really day and night; I don't believe I can get off." Instead, he sent his best representative—his wife, First Lady Eleanor. She had been interested in the Bonus Marchers, keeping up with their story in the newspapers. One day, without letting her know where she was going, an FDR advisor asked her to go on a drive with him installing safety railings and electric lights. They carried out irrigation and water reclamation projects and built earthen dams. They stocked streams with fish and made improvements at many Civil War battlefields. In Alaska some CCC members of the Tlingit Indian tribe restored totem poles.

However, although great results were achieved by the CCC in making improvements in the nation's parks, the program had little impact on the overall economy. The Corps did provide the U.S. Army with a pool from which to recruit future non-commissioned officers, but critics of the CCC

around Washington. He drove to the Bonus Marchers' camp and told her that Franklin wanted her to talk to the vets. It had been 10 months since General MacArthur had ordered the Anacostia Flats camp destroyed. The First Lady was anxious and uncertain how she might be received.

Writing later, Eleanor addressed her concerns: "Very hesitatingly, I got out and walked over to where I saw a line-up of men waiting for food. They looked me over curiously, and one of them asked my name and what I wanted. When I said I just wanted to see how they were getting on, they asked me to join them." Soon, everyone in the camp knew the First Lady was there. She slogged around the camp, getting mud all over her shoes, as it had rained earlier. She sat down and ate with them in one of the mess halls and talked about a visit she had made with doughboys in France back in 1919. They made her feel at home, she made them feel appreciated. Before she left, the First Lady led a group of Marchers in several old soldier songs.

It was all such a far cry from the way they had been treated the previous summer. As Eleanor left, the Bonus men wished her good luck, and she said "Good-bye and good luck to you!" One vet summed it all up: "Hoover sent the army; Roosevelt sent his wife." In the end, President Roosevelt did not sign the bonus for the vets, but he did offer them jobs in his new Civilian Conservation Corps. By June 1933, 2,600 of them had signed up.

always fretted that the program was too "militaristic." It was a public relations success, though. One of the most enduring images of the New Deal became the youthful CCC workers, shirtless, their belts cinched tight, proudly carrying shovels to their next work site.

Today it is a rare national or even state park that does not still bear the marks of contributions made by the hard-working boys of the CCC. Many elderly men recall their days in the CCC as some of the best of their lives. One CCC vet recalled how "It made a man of me all right." Another knew at the time the value of the CCC: "If a boy wants to go and get a job after he's been in the C's, he'll know how to work."

REDIRECTING THE CAMPAIGN

As the early weeks of the Roosevelt administration passed, later proposals sent to Congress took a turn in another direction. Leading the way in the redirection of the New Deal were a handful of advisors to the president, who included Professor Rexford G. Tugwell, Raymond Moley, and Adolph A. Berle, Jr. They believed that the government would gain by allowing businesses to consolidate to survive, even as the government established national economic standards and regulations. To that end these New Dealers called for the establishment of two major reform agencies—the National Recovery Administration (NRA) and the Public Works Administration (PWA).

An Agency for Economic Planning

When Congress passed the National Industrial Recovery Act (NIRA), which created the NRA, President Roosevelt referred to it as "the most important and far-reaching legislation ever passed by the American Congress." The larger purpose of the NIRA was to drive prices up and, as FDR himself said, "put people back to work." At its core, the NRA sought to establish a different relationship between the nation's industrial and business sector and the federal government. The NRA exerted almost dictatorial power over U.S. business. While businesses were encouraged to "voluntarily" cooperate with the NRA, the government put pressure on those who tried to hold out.

First Lady Eleanor Roosevelt inspects work at a Works Progress Administration (WPA) project site. The WPA was run by Harry Hopkins. He built it into the largest employer in the country.

The NRA's overarching purpose was to solve the problems of economic instability, overproduction, and labor-management issues by carrying out economic planning. Representing industrial leaders, labor leaders, and government bureaucrats, the NRA created new "codes" of competition. The codes were based on limiting production while setting prices and workers' hours and wages. Of the 700 or more NRA codes, approximately 58 included price-fixing clauses. The strict rules of capitalism took a back seat to the latent socialism of the NRA.

The head of the NRA was General Hugh S. "Ironpants" Johnson, who was appointed by FDR. Johnson was an army vet, a West Point graduate, who had campaigned in Mexico before World War I with George Patton during Pershing's punitive expedition to capture Pancho Villa. Through his hard work and tedious planning, Johnson launched the NRA with fanfare and public support. Johnson was gruff and tyrannical. When asked by a reporter what would happen to those who did not agree to abide by the NRA codes, he answered matter-of-factly, notes historian William Manchester: "They'll get a sock right on the nose."

The Blue Eagle

By July 1933, 500 U.S. industrial businesses had signed NRA codes, affecting 22 million employees. By the end of that summer, the nation's 10 largest industries had joined up, along with countless hundreds of smaller businesses—everything from breweries to mom-and-pop stores. When a business agreed to cooperate with the NRA, it received posters to display in its store window. These featured the NRA's symbol, a blue eagle grasping lightning bolts and a set of industrial gears in its talons. The signs told would-be customers which businesses were working with the NRA, and which ones were not. The government's assumption was that Americans would not do business with uncooperative companies or storefronts.

The NRA's goals may have been well intentioned, but its tenure was a short one. Johnson proved to be too forceful: He overreacted to those who did not abide by the NRA's guidelines. Sometimes the general's actions were little more than browbeating and name-calling. Big businessmen dominated the NRA boards, and sometimes set up systems that favored them at the expense of smaller businesses. Without enough personnel, the NRA could not keep up with the sheer scope of the business sector, and many businesses simply ignored the agency. Others did not like how much power the NRA had over them and the extent to which the agency tried to tell them how to run their businesses. The NRA did have its successes and accomplishments, including setting labor codes that banned child labor, and establishing minimum wages and maximum hours, which were advantageous to the working class. Yet labor unions sometimes opposed NRA guidelines because the agency often set wages below the level union members wanted.

Building Across America

The act that created the NRA also tried to "prime the pump" of industrial recovery by supporting large public works projects, which would provide jobs. The result was the establishment of the Public Works Administration (PWA), which, like the NRA, sought industrial recovery and unemployment relief. The agency was established on the assumption that spending on public works would help fix the economy. Roosevelt appointed Harold Ickes, the administration's secretary of the interior and former Bull Moose Party supporter, to run the program.

The act appropriated $3.3 billion for tens of thousands of building projects. Between 1933 and 1939, the PWA spent a total of $6 billion and invested 4.75 billion man-hours of labor. During those years it built 10 percent of all the nation's new transportation facilities, 35 percent of the hospitals and health facilities, 65 percent of the new city halls, courthouses, and sewage disposal plants, and 70 percent of all educational buildings.

Some of New York City's most significant building projects of the era were constructed with PWA monies, including the Triborough Bridge, the Lincoln Tunnel, and La Guardia Airport. Other PWA projects included Virginia's Skyline Drive, the Washington, D.C. Zoo, the gold depository at Fort Knox, the Overseas Highway in the Florida Keys, and the San Francisco-Oakland Bay Bridge in California. Even military projects, such as the aircraft carriers *Yorktown* and *Enterprise,* were constructed by the PWA, along with the light cruiser *Vincennes,* built in the Bethlehem Steel shipyard in Quincy, Massachusetts.

Perhaps the largest construction project of the PWA was the building of the Grand Coulee Dam on the Columbia River. The Grand Coulee represented the grandest structure in scope, perhaps since the building of the Great Wall of China. It seemed to some critics a crazy thing to build: a dam capable of producing water reservoirs to irrigate millions of acres of farmland at a time when the government was starting to pay farmers not to produce too much. But the project provided electricity for the Pacific Northwest and irrigation for 500,000 acres (200,000 hectares) of the Columbia Valley. At the time, the Grand Coulee Dam was the largest concrete structure in the country.

Help for Home Owners

Roosevelt's New Deal soon became a complicated package of answers to meet the challenges of the Depression. One of the looming issues was the state of the home mortgage industry. Home foreclosures had become so commonplace that they were occurring at a rate of 1,000 a day when Roosevelt took office. His New Deal sought to address this crisis by pushing through Congress an act called the Home Owners' Loan Corporation (HOLC). This agency sought to provide security for home owners by issuing government bonds to help refinance more than 1 million house mortgages. Over the next two years the HOLC spent $3 billion and managed to save 10 percent of the country's mortgaged homes from default or foreclosure.

In 1934 Congress also created the Federal Housing Administration (FHA) which offered long-term mortgages along with lower payment requirements. Since such New Deal agencies as the HOLC and FHA provided support for single-family dwellings, they also helped further a trend of growth in the suburbs rather than the inner cities.

4

Extending the Reach

For most of those Americans who experienced the Great Depression, the 1930s represented the beginning. But many farm incomes had already dropped off during the 1920s, giving farmers a head start into bad times. In 1932 farmers were receiving 25 cents for a bushel of wheat, 7 cents for a bushel of corn, 10 cents for oats, a nickel for a pound of Southern cotton. A pound of sugar yielded 3 cents, beef and pork, 2.5 cents a pound. And a box of 200 good apples might be worth 40 cents. With mortgage interest at $3.60 an acre, along with taxes at nearly $2 per acre, wheat producers lost $1.50 for each acre grown. The last time farmers could remember flush times was during the years just prior to and during World War I. During the Depression the nation's farmers, dairymen, and ranchers dreamed of "parity," which would have valued their produce—whether hogs, corn, milk, or other farm products—at a price relative to industrial prices as they had stood in 1914.

ELECTRICITY FOR THE FARM

But other difficulties plagued the farm industry, many of which had always been the bane of life for those who lived in rural regions. Even in 1935 the vast majority of America's farms still operated without electricity. Machines on the farm were hand-operated or ran on steam-power or gasoline-powered generators, often called "hired men" by farmers. Power companies had long estimated the cost of rural electrification as too high, perhaps $5,000 per mile (1.6 km) of electric line strung.

Intent on placing the government in the arena of electrification, Roosevelt pushed through Congress a bill creating the Tennessee Valley Authority (TVA). His goal was to target an underprivileged, even backward region of the United States—poverty-stricken Appalachia—and bring it into the twentieth century. The region, including eastern Tennessee and parts of Georgia, Alabama, and North Carolina, was home to several major river basins, such as the Tennessee and its many tributaries. Through the TVA, the federal government approved the construction of 21 dams along the river system to provide flood control and produce hydroelectric power for tens of thousands of farms and coal mining villages. The act was passed in May 1933 as part of the Hundred Days.

Two years later FDR issued an executive order that brought about the Rural Electrification Administration (REA), whose purpose was to string the electric lines in farming regions that private industry had for so many years claimed would be too large-scale and too expensive a project. All along the dirt roads of rural America, electric poles were raised and wires strung. Over the next seven years—1935 to 1942—rural areas were lit up with electricity for the first time. Farmhouses gained electrical lights and other conveniences, while farm operations used the power to run everything from milking machines to grain dryers. Electricity was such a new phenomenon for the farming community that one Texas family, relates historian James Kirby Martin, saw a house lit up one night, and the mother shouted out: "Oh my God, the house is on fire." Her daughter corrected her: "No Mamma. The lights are on."

THE AGRICULTURE ADJUSTMENT ACT

In addition to electrification, rural Americans received benefits from several new federal agencies. The Soil Conservation Service helped farmers fight soil erosion, the Farm Credit Administration helped with limited relief from foreclosure, and the Commodity Credit Corporation allowed farmers to secure loans by using stored farm produce as collateral. But the most far-reaching New Deal legislation directed to help farmers was the Agriculture Adjustment Act (AAA).

The AAA program was set up to make the government a major player in the U.S. commodities market. The government would actively work to reduce the amount of farm goods produced annually, thus causing a rise in prices. FDR's secretary of agriculture, Henry Wallace, working closely with farmers, helped organize "domestic allotment" plans that would set a benchmark limit on the produce yielded from a certain number of acres. On a voluntary basis, growers who cut their production to match the established quotas would be paid by the government for making the cuts, which sometimes called for some acreage to be left unsown. Government payments, or subsidies, would be paid for through a tax placed on food-processing middlemen—those who purchased from the farmer and placed the produce in the consumer market. This allowed the AAA to support itself.

The plan was innovative and extremely controversial. Since the act was part of the Hundred Days, crops had already been planted, and animal populations were already in existence. Under those conditions, southern farmers were paid $100 million to cut 10 million acres (4 million ha) of cotton and leave it in the fields. Six million young hogs were killed, along with 200,000 pregnant sows, representing 9 million pounds (4 million kilograms) of meat. Only 1 million lbs (453,000 kg) of this were taken by the government and handed out to needy people. To many Americans, the waste seemed disgraceful. During the years that followed,

Migrant workers on the road in Crittenden County, Arkansas, in 1936. Sometimes they would get picked up on the road by a farm truck and taken many miles for a day's work. Then they were back on the road.

the AAA did not have to go to such extremes, but the bad taste of 1933 remained for many. The AAA had gained a reputation as a destroyer of food.

Otherwise the AAA made some inroads toward better farm prices. During its first four farming seasons agriculture prices doubled. Still, the AAA did not ultimately solve the problems of overproduction. Farmers had become so good at raising food—due to mechanization and chemical fertilizers—that they continued to grow too much of it to stabilize prices. As for parity, in 1933 farm prices reached 55 percent parity and in 1936 they reached upward to 90 percent.

Not everyone benefited from the agency. Southern sharecroppers and tenant farmers, most of whom were black, did not benefit because they did not own their own land. If those who did own the land signed on and agreed not to produce on all their available acres, they let their workers go, leaving them in worse situations. A total of 50,000 tenant families were cut loose. Between 1932 and 1935, 3 million farmers stopped farming and moved to urban areas in search of jobs and a new start.

1934: NEW POLICIES

While the New Deal had put down deep roots during FDR's Hundred Days, there were more programs yet to come. In November 1933 the Civil Works Administration (CWA) was established with Harry Hopkins, a social programs organizer from New York, at the helm. This program was designed to put the unemployed to work. During Hopkins' first two hours on the job he doled out $5 million in relief funds to begin the program's various work projects. Before the end of the year the CWA had put 2.6 million men to work, and by early 1934 the number was up to 4 million. Much of this work was manual labor, building 250,000 miles (400,000 km) of roads, 40,000 schools, 150,000 restroom facilities, and 3,700 playgrounds. But FDR did not keep the program long term, worried that he would be creating a class of workers who were dependent on artificial job programs provided by the government.

During 1934 the initial programs of the New Deal only had a limited impact on the overall economy. While some problems, such as the banking crisis, had been stabilized, the economic downturn continued to deepen. Some labor organizations ordered their workers to strike, which sometimes descended into violence. American Communists tried to rally farm workers. A broad-based strike in San Francisco nearly shut down the city for four days. Discontent stretched from coast to coast. A Labor Day strike was called, producing the largest work stoppage in U.S. history.

Many voices called for Roosevelt to do something—do more, do something different. The 1934 Congressional elections seemed to give him a further mandate. The Democrats won 13 new House seats, as well as nine new Senate seats, with most of those newly elected having campaigned for further government reform of the economy. Only one-third of the Congress was still Republican and only seven states were still led by Republicans. Harry Hopkins, the former head of the CWA, excitedly announced to his fellow Democrats, notes historian William Manchester: "Boys—this is our hour. We've got to get everything we want—a works program, social security, wages and hours, everything—now or never. Get your minds to work on developing a complete ticket to provide security for all the folks of this country up and down and across the board."

The Influence of Keynes
With the two-year elections behind him Roosevelt looked forward to a fresh run of New Deal programs and strategies. FDR had said from the beginning that his strategy in battling

the Depression would be "bold, persistent experimentation." The year 1934 would be no different. After a year in office he was prepared to abandon his previous hopes that he would be able to maintain a balanced budget. A British economist, John Maynard Keynes, had visited the White House in the spring of 1934 and explained to FDR the benefits of deficit spending. Keynes had sent a letter to the president fol-

An ex-farmer and worker for the Work Projects Administration with his child outside their living quarters—a shack—in Circleville, Ohio. This photograph was taken August 1938.

lowing his Hundred Days, a critique of those New Deal acts that had been implemented by that time, notes historian H.W. Brands:

> *You have made yourself the trustee for those in every country who seek to mend the evils of our condition by reasoned experiment within the framework of the existing social system… [I]f you succeed, new and bolder methods will be tried everywhere, and we may date the first chapter of a new economic era from your accession to office.*

Keynes claimed that the Depression would never be tamed nor a full recovery achieved until the U.S. government set a course of spending that included annual deficits of $300 million. After creating a strategy based on government planning, while working alongside the business sector, the president was now ready to meet the Depression head on with massive government spending.

THE WORKS PROGRESS ADMINISTRATION

One of Roosevelt's first significant programs of the New Year went on line in January. The Works Progress Administration—renamed the Works Projects Administration in 1939—was financed with $5 billion and its goal was to provide jobs for 3.5 million Americans with pay that represented a "security wage." That amount was double the existing welfare payment level, but it was still much lower than expected by members of a typical U.S. union. Once more, FDR tapped Harry Hopkins to direct the program. Much of the work of the WPA amounted to construction projects, such as the building or improving of 2,500 hospitals, nearly 6,000 schools, 1,000 airports, and 13,000 playgrounds. Such work was hands-on, with concrete results that often improved the lives of those living in the communities where the new facilities were located. But WPA workers did not just build hospitals and schools; they manned them. Some worked in school cafeterias, where they served one million school lunches daily.

Workers of all Professions

The program also hired workers for "light construction" projects, especially those related to the arts. Many of those recruited for WPA work were paid up to $94.90 a month. WPA workers included artists, actors, writers, musicians, and photographers, who applied their talents to the needs of the program.

If a post office was built by WPA construction workers, for example, unemployed artists might be hired through the WPA's Art Project to paint a mural in the post office lobby. WPA painters who would one day become famous included Jackson Pollock, Willem de Kooning, and Ben Shahn. In Chicago the lobby of the Cook County Hospital included WPA murals painted by Edwin Boyd Johnson, WPA mosaic murals by John Winter, a WPA statue by Charles Umlauf, and polished stone benches carved by WPA-employed stonecutters. Along the slopes of Oregon's Mount Hood, near Portland, WPA workers constructed the Timberline Lodge to enhance a new ski resort, its coffee shop decorated with a mural by WPA artist Douglas Lynch. Patrons of the coffee shop sat on sturdy wooden chairs carved by WPA craftsmen.

WPA workers came in all stripes and professions. Members of a city symphony might become WPA musicians if their city government could no longer afford to support them. Musicians played in local parades and between innings at baseball games. There were WPA folk performers, brass bands, and cowboy balladeers. In the spring of 1936 San Diego's WPA Federal Civic Opera Company performed seven free concerts of Mascagni's *Cavalleria Rusticana* at the

Russ Auditorium. The opera performers were accompanied by the WPA's Federal Philharmonic Orchestra and the WPA chorus of 50 singers. All the performers—the operatic company and the chorus—wore costumes fashioned by WPA seamstresses.

Writers, Photographers, and Actors

WPA writers and photographers toured the country and recorded what they saw. They worked in parallel with the Farm Security Agency (FSA), which employed dozens of photographers, including Dorothea Lange, Walker Evans, and even artist Ben Shahn, to document with their cameras life in America during the Depression. The result was a series of photo publications called *I've Seen America,* compendiums of people and places across the country. All told, the WPA and FSA photographers shot 27,000 photographs, sometimes showing the desperate lives of many victims of the Depression. However, out of all that documentary camera work, only a small number of pictures showed Americans without hope, or those broken by the economy. Most of those pictured were framed as survivors who had made it through difficulty and adversity.

Another WPA arts group was the Federal Writers Project, which produced a variety of state, city, and small town guidebooks, while other writers went out and collected old stories, folk tales, and other Americana. Former slaves were interviewed, sometimes tape recorded, and their histories written down, salvaging important oral histories from America's past. Sometimes, WPA writers just wrote about the WPA itself, to help advertise the agency's successes and advancements. Young writers employed by the WPA included John Cheever, Zora Neale Hurston, Studs Terkel, Saul Bellow, and black writers such as Ralph Ellison and Richard Wright. One of California writer John Steinbeck's jobs with the WPA was to count all the dogs on Monterey Peninsula. Likewise, musicologists traveled around, looking for folk music to record and preserve. Woody Guthrie was one musician who was interviewed by WPA workers, his music recorded and produced in three record albums.

The WPA Theatre Project presented live stage productions and something called the "living newspaper," which was

THE WPA FROM COAST TO COAST

Under the leadership of Harry Hopkins, the Works Progress Administration employed everyone from construction workers to artists. Ultimately, hundreds of thousands of projects were carried out under the auspices of the WPA, and these could be found everywhere across the United States.

In New York City one of the most important WPA projects was the refurbishment of the Statue of Liberty. The work took place over 20 months with improvements costing $250,000. Over the decades rainwater had worn at the statue's pedestal, so in 1937 WPA crews added metal flashing to redirect the water. In addition, the statue's internal steel framework was repainted, the spikes in the Lady Liberty's crown were reinforced, the torch repaired, a new staircase installed, and extensive landscaping was added to the grounds on Bedloe's Island. The new and improved Statue of Liberty was reopened to the public in December 1938.

Meanwhile, out on the West Coast, San Francisco's new Aquatic Park near Fisherman's Wharf was dedicated the following month. Another WPA project, the park had cost $1.5 million. The facility provided a place for such water-related activities as boating and swimming. There were new grandstands that looked out over downtown San Francisco's only beachfront, alongside a modernist new building that included restaurants, the whole complex adorned by several WPA murals. Through its nearly two years of construction, the park had employed 782 workers and artists.

performed to provide audiences with information on everyday life in America. All told, the Federal Theatre entertained nearly 30 million people with shows around the country.

"Make Work" Projects

There were failures within the WPA. Some jobs, known as "make work" projects, accomplished little or had no apparent purpose. Workmen might be hired to move a pile of dirt from one place to another, for example. Sometimes workers had little to actually do on a job site, leaving them to be paid to do nothing more than lean on their shovels. Such circumstances caused critics of the program to assert that the letters WPA stood for "We Piddle Around."

A common claim was that anyone working for the WPA automatically slipped into a state of suspended animation. The jokes sometimes flew at the WPA's expense, such as the tale of two old guys, one asking the other how old he was. "Eighty-four," his friend answers. "I would have been eighty-six, but I was on WPA for two years." Trumpeter Louis Armstrong and the singing group, the Mills Brothers, recorded a hit song for Decca Records with lyrics that included: "Sleep while you work while you rest while you play/Lean on your shovel to pass the time away."

Yet ultimately, thousands of writers, actors, artists, and others did find employment through the Works Progress Administration. Despite those who sometimes derided the program, the WPA would long be remembered for its legacy of significant projects—construction, artistic, and otherwise—that remain a part of the U.S. landscape even today.

5

The Second Hundred Days

The WPA represented the high point of Roosevelt's power to influence Congress and see his proposals through to reality. After that bill passed, Congress became less cooperative in response to increasing voices of opposition. The National Recovery Administration was not universally popular, and conservatives claimed it subverted capitalism. From the other side, liberals chastised FDR for not doing enough to help the poor.

Roosevelt's New Deal was bound to have its critics, of course. Such radical changes in the uses of federal power to alter the nation's economy would always be controversial. Roosevelt had said early on: "Let's concentrate upon one thing. Save the people and the nation and, if we have to change our minds twice a day to accomplish that end, we should do it." Sometimes even those directly involved in establishing New Deal programs were critical of one another's suggestions or economic philosophies. Many times those disagreements were kept under wraps, with the public unaware of the feuding.

VOICES OF OPPOSITION

What could not be kept under wraps were the sometimes loud voices of public opposition, which came from a variety of camps. While the opponents were many, three men took the forefront—a senator from Louisiana, a Catholic priest, and a retired medical doctor.

Huey Long: Share the Wealth

Perhaps the loudest and most colorful opponent was Senator Huey Long of Louisiana. The former governor despised Roosevelt and his New Deal and was highly critical of the NRA and the AAA. As an alternative, he promoted a plan of his own, a get-rich-quick scheme for the majority of Americans that he called his "Share the Wealth" plan.

Long claimed that the nation's real economic problem was an uneven distribution of wealth. His idea was to force anyone with wealth greater than $5 million to pay that additional amount through a capital tax. He would then put an income tax law in place that forbade any American from earning more than $1 million annually. With the money generated from taxing the wealthy, Long promised every American enough to spend $5,000 to buy land and a house, plus a car and a home radio. Pensions would be handed out to elderly citizens, and those young people considered "worthy" would be sent to college free of charge. As icing on the cake, Long promised huge public works projects across the country, with workers paid a federally mandated minimum wage, and a 30-hour workweek.

By February 1935 Long's "Share the Wealth" clubs boasted 27,000 members. His slogan was "every man a king, but no man wears a crown." Long became so popular with some groups that in 1935 he announced he would stand as a presidential candidate in 1936. That never happened, however: Long was assassinated on September 10, 1935, by the son-in-law of one of his critics.

Father Coughlin: Radio Diatribes

Another of Roosevelt's opponents was Father Charles E. Coughlin, a Catholic priest from Royal Oak, Michigan. Coughlin used his national radio program, which reached between 30 and 40 million people, to criticize the New Deal, which he called the "Pagan Deal." Father Coughlin accused the Roosevelt administration alternatively of supporting Wall Street capitalists at the expense of the public and of cozying up to Communists. The priest wanted Roosevelt to nationalize the banks and inflate the currency to provide people with greater spending power.

In 1934 Coughlin established the National Union for Social Justice, gaining support from lower-middle-class Americans, especially ethnic Catholics in the Northeast and the Midwest. He claimed that 7.5 million followers had signed up to join this organization. His radio diatribes criticized bankers and union leaders and favored the average working-class American and small business owners. At times Coughlin's message was anti-semitic, as he twisted the New Deal into the "Jew Deal."

Dr. Townsend: Old Age Pensions

Out in California Roosevelt's critics included Dr. Francis E. Townsend, whose complaints were driven less by personal ambition and more by personal philosophy. Townsend had served as the public health officer in Long Beach until he lost his job at age 67 with almost no money in his savings. Seeing many others in situations similar to his (on one occasion he was especially moved at the sight of three elderly women scavenging for food out of garbage cans), he developed an old age relief plan that reflected, to an extent, programs that already existed in some European countries.

Townsend announced his "Old Age Revolving Pensions, Limited" in January 1934. This plan proposed that each person over the age of 60 would receive a pension of $200 each month. In exchange, those elderly citizens had to retire and agree to spend all the money they received each month in

A cartoon, "The Three Musketeers," shows New Deal critics Gerald L.K. Smith—an associate of the late Senator Huey Long—Francis E. Townsend, and Father Charles Edward Coughlin. They were uncertain who should lead their new Union Party for the 1936 presidential campaign. The party was soon disbanded.

the United States, which would help stimulate and feed the U.S. economy. The program would also mean that jobs formerly held by the elderly would be open to younger workers. Critics only had to look at the numbers to determine

What Americans Earned, 1932–34

For the twenty-first-century American, it is difficult to understand how much different salaries were for workers when compared to today's average incomes. With a national minimum wage today of over $7 an hour (translating to an annual income of $14,000 based on a 40-hour workweek), was a wage in 1932 of, say, $2,500, much money or not? To provide perspective, the following list presents salaries typical for specific types of work performed in the United States for years 1932 to 1934.

Airline pilot: $8,000
Live-in maid: $260
Airline stewardess: $1,500
Mayor (city of 30-50,000) $2,317
Pharmaceutical salesmen: $1,500
Bituminous coal miner: $723
Police chief $2,636
Bus driver: $1,373
Priest: $831
Chauffeur: $624
Public school teacher: $1,227

Civil Service engineer: $1,284
Publicity agent: $1,800
College professor: $3,111
Railroad executive: $5,064
Construction worker: $907
Railroad conductor: $2,729
Dentist: $2,391
Registered nurse: $936
Department store model: $936
Secretary: $1,040
Doctor: $3,382
Statistician: $1,820
Dressmaker: $780
Steelworker: $422
Electrical worker: $1,559
Stenographer-bookkeeper: $936
Engineer: $2,520
Textile worker: $435
Fire Chief (city of 30-50,000):$2,075
Typist: $624
Hired farm hand: $216
United States Congressman: $8,663
Housemother-Boy's school: $780
Waitress: $520
Lawyer: $4,218

that Townsend's scheme would not work properly. The program would cost $24 billion of the federal government's $40 billion annual income, but would provide pensions for less than 10 percent of the U.S. population. When confronted with such statistics, Townsend's answer was simple, notes historian James Kirby Martin: "I am not in the least interested in the cost of the plan."

MORE NEW DEAL

While these opponents and critics might not have had viable alternative answers to the problems Roosevelt was trying to tackle with his New Deal, the president could not simply ignore them. Such men might represent the opinions of millions of Americans. This type of criticism—and there were many more critics across the country—began to work on FDR, causing him to abandon all hope of uniting the entire country behind his New Deal proposals. Instead, he chose to move away from conservative limitations, taking his programs to the left.

By 1935 Roosevelt was developing a further batch of proposals and programs that would later be referred to as his "Second Hundred Days." Despite its name, the Second Hundred Days lasted a total of 177 days. Two acts dominated the new batch of legislation—the National Labor Relations Act and the Social Security bill.

The National Labor Relations Act

This new law derived from a bill presented by New York Senator Robert F. Wagner, and was popularly known as the Wagner Act. It was meant to replace a section of the NIRA regarding labor. To that point, FDR had not made any significant shift in the government's policy concerning labor, but the Wagner Act changed that. Swept through Congress with large majorities, the act guaranteed workers the right

Unionized strikers fight with a group of "scabs" or nonunion replacement employees as they try to cross the picket line at a factory. The strikers regarded the scabs as Fascists, who opposed the government's employment strategies.

to organize a labor union and created the National Labor Relations Board (NLRB), which could come down hard on businesses that carried out "unfair labor practices."

The natural result of the act was a dramatic increase in the number of unions and in union membership. In the steel, textile, and automobile industries, workers rallied, took advantage of the opportunity to bargain collectively, and engaged in labor stoppages. "Sit down" strikes in December 1937 at General Motors' Fisher Plant No. 2 in Detroit and Plant No. 1 in Flint saw workers refusing to leave their factories and locking out management. This led to police intervention, with automobile workers lobbing at the police, notes Foster Rhea Dulles, anything they could get their hands on, including "coffee mugs, pop bottles, iron bolts, and heavy automobile door hinges." The strike was a success for the auto workers, who won a 10 percent wage increase and reduction to an eight-hour workday, 40-hour workweek.

That same year membership of the United Auto Workers union increased from 30,000 to more than 400,000, while the Steel Workers' Organizing Committee added 350,000 new members. The Wagner Act had provided a new framework of security and confidence for hundreds of thousands of U.S. workers.

Social Security

Following the NLRA came the Social Security bill. Since the days of the Progressive movement a generation earlier, the living conditions and financial security of America's elderly had been of concern. They had always been viewed as the "visible poor," and their numbers included not just the elderly, but dependent children and the handicapped. Again New York Senator Wagner sponsored the bill, along with Congressman David Lewis of Pennsylvania. Roosevelt signed it on August 15, 1935.

In one fell swoop, the federal government took the wind out of Dr. Townsend's sails by establishing a system by which workers aged over 65 years would receive monthly stipends on the basis of their life earnings, with payments beginning in 1940. It also gave out small relief checks to older people living in poverty. All this was to be financed through a contributory system of payroll taxes, paid by both workers and their employers. In a sense, this was something new for the federal government, but the idea was borrowed from similar state programs. By the mid-1930s, 29 of the 48 states had already established old-age pension programs.

TENNESSEE VALLEY AUTHORITY

The TVA was set up in 1933 mainly to boost the economy in areas badly hit by the Great Depression. Dams were built along major rivers in the area to provide electricity for both public and private industries. Today, the TVA is the nation's largest public supplier of electricity.

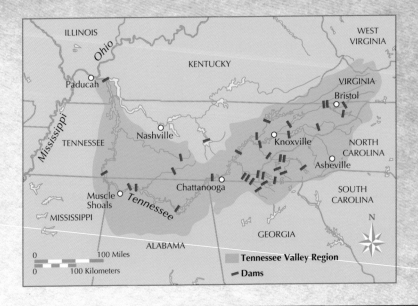

The Social Security program also included Aid to Dependent Children (ADC), which provided monies for poor mothers and their dependents. This program paid federal matching monies to the states, each of which would operate its own program. Recipients of federal aid were now considered social dependents of the federal government.

Although the new law was lauded by some as a sign of the federal government's intent to use power to provide some groups of Americans with a social safety net, others were critical. The payments to the elderly were small, ranging from $10 to $85 a month, and the program left out many groups, including migrant workers, civil servants, and employees of religious organizations. Conservatives railed that the law represented little more than socialism.

Indeed, through this and additional acts the government was becoming the final support for the aged, disabled, and dependent, and even the unemployed. For the first time in U.S. history, citizens were looking to the government with a sense of entitlement; that it was government's *responsibility* to provide supports for its people. It was a role FDR accepted, especially in the case of Social Security. He once bragged that "no damn politician can ever scrap my social security program." He could not have been more right. Over the decades since, Social Security has become one of the most protected systems managed by the federal government.

Experimenting With the Economic System

The President's Second Hundred Days saw additional legislation, such as regulations on utilities, further banking reform, and new taxes. There was the Soil Conservation Act, a stronger Federal Reserve Board, and the Rural Electrification Act. A variation on the CCC was created—the National Youth Administration—designed to provide jobs for youths from families on relief, including part-time employment for needy college students. None of these moves—including Social Security—was meant to change the fundamental political and economic systems in America. Several of the acts actually supported capitalism, while making the system appear more caring. While it had always been FDR's goal to "experiment" with the economic system and the role of government, he had never intended to scrap capitalism or even monkey with the basic elements of democracy.

The same could not be said of other western industrial nations during the early 1930s. Just weeks before FDR took office in early March 1933 the people of Germany, their nation racked by the Depression, had witnessed the appointment of a new chancellor, one who would meet his country's economic problems by establishing a socialist state at the expense of capitalism, while laying the seeds of tyranny—Adolf Hitler.

THE COURT WEIGHS IN

By 1935 earlier New Deal programs were coming under fire from a new, powerful front—the U.S. Supreme Court. On May 27 the Court decided against the NRA in a case cited *Schechter Poultry Corporation v. United States*, which was always referred to afterward as the "sick chicken" case.

The Schechter family were longstanding kosher butchers in Brooklyn, who had not abided by the requirements of the NRA codes. NRA officials had tried to make a case against the Schechters, accusing them of flagrantly violating NRA guidelines concerning price and wage fixing, as well as disregarding the agency's maximum work hours rule and the right of its workers to unionize. The agency also accused the Schechters of selling sick poultry, which broke additional NRA health codes. Initially, 60 charges were laid against Schechter Poultry, later reduced to 18, including "the sale to a butcher of an unfit chicken."

In its ruling, the Supreme Court decided against the NRA. In fact, government lawyers never proved that the Schechters had ever sold a "sick chicken." The Court's decision was significant since it declared the National Industrial Recovery Act (NIRA) of 1933 unconstitutional. This was on the grounds that the legislation and the codes the NIRA instituted violated the constitutional separation of powers by handing off an unlawful portion of legislative power to the executive branch. Also, the Court held that NIRA provisions had gone beyond the power of Congress itself. As a result, the NIRA, and thus the NRA, were dead.

Changing Acts

The Supreme Court also struck down other parts of the New Deal, including the Agricultural Adjustment Act (AAA). On January 6, 1936, the Court ruled by a vote of six to three that the AAA was unconstitutional. Chief Justice Roberts, arguing for the majority, stated that farming was not a national activity and that states, not the federal government, should have jurisdiction over the agricultural activities within their borders. At the heart of the decision, though, the Court declared that the AAA's regulatory taxation provisions were unconstitutional. In the aftermath of the AAA's demise, the New Deal Congress quickly passed the Soil Conservation and Domestic Allotment Act of 1936 as an alternative.

The U.S. court system gave the New Deal a drubbing in 1934, with individual judges filing injunctions against some of the new federal laws. More than 1,000 cases concerning New Deal laws were in litigation that year. One of the problems was the overreach of the Roosevelt administration. In addition, only three out of every 10 federal judges were fellow Democrats. On the Supreme Court, the average age of the justices was 78, and the majority of them were conservative.

WEATHERING THE DEPRESSION

The Great Depression of the 1930s delivered its own versions of misery and economic malaise, on a scale never experienced before in U.S. history. Across the country economic victims of every background, class, race, and philosophy abounded. Yet as bad as the economy was during the early 1930s, life was made even more unbearable for many Americans by the weather.

In the mid-1930s floods became commonplace as the nation's major rivers—the Mississippi, Ohio, Potomac, Tennessee, Missouri, Susquehanna, Columbia, and others—overflowed their banks, causing massive destruction. Thousands died during such catastrophes. The 1937 flood along the Ohio River corridor was the worst in recorded U.S. history, and left half a million people homeless. In addition, winters were extremely cold, while summers reached sweltering temperatures. During the summer of 1936 residents of Kansas experienced 60 days of temperatures of more than 100°F (37.7°C).

The Dust Bowl

Perhaps, however, no weather circumstances delivered more desolation to the United States than the long-term drought that spread across the Great Plains and the resulting clouds of dust that rose up and engulfed millions of Americans. This was the age of the Dust Bowl, when gale-force winds swept the drought-stricken farm fields of the Midwest, lifting millions of pounds of topsoil toward the heavens and creating "black blizzards."

For years conservationists, soil management experts, and even some farmers themselves had predicted the ecological disaster of great dust clouds spreading across the Plains. A century earlier American explorers had dubbed the Plains as the "Great American Desert" and this was never more true

LEAVING THE DUST BOWL

The Dust Bowl was an area that encompassed the prairies of both the United States and Canada. Within it, most of the soil had turned to dust and been blow away by strong winds. The dust was blown eastward and southward, settling on cities along the East Coast and reaching far out into the Atlantic Ocean. The dust choked people and livestock, vehicle engines, and farm machinery. More than 500,000 people were made homeless and, by 1940, more than 2.5 million people had left the area to settle elsewhere. Many of them moved to California to find work and new homes, but they often found themselves in competition with unemployed migrants from elsewhere.

A family in Kansas fixes its car as it prepares to abandon its farm destroyed by drought and windstorms.

than during the 1930s. Endless expansion of farming in the region, with its overplowing and overgrazing, had removed the prairie grasses that had held the soil in place for thousands of years. A decade earlier 100 counties on the Plains—in states including Colorado, Kansas, New Mexico, Texas, and Oklahoma—had already begun to see the great clouds of dust rising up. By the 1930s the problem had reached epic

In 1934, at the height of the drought, a "black blizzard" hits the town of Lamar in Colorado. The dark clouds of dust often turned day into night and people complained of being able to see no more than a few feet in front of them.

proportions. The storms became so severe that some people believed they signaled the end of the world and Christ's Second Coming.

Such organizations as the National Resources Board estimated that, in 1934 alone, the effects of the Dust Bowl destroyed 35 million acres (14 million ha) of Great Plains farmland, while placing another 225 million acres (91 million ha) in critical condition. The 100 victim counties quickly grew to more than 750.

Black Whirlwinds

The Roosevelt administration saw its first great dust storms on Armistice Day of 1933, when the winds began to blow in South Dakota and the sky turned dark as night. People breathed in dust until they actually vomited dirt. When the storms passed, farm fields were covered with dust and sand. Great dunes of topsoil lay piled up alongside barns and houses, covering farm machinery. Roads disappeared. As the wind pushed the dust along, cities from Minneapolis to Chicago to Albany, New York were shrouded in black whirlwinds.

And the winds continued throughout 1934 and into 1935. It all produced conditions of extremes—too much wind and dust; not enough snow, rain, or earth-containing grasses. The storms spread out like locust across a wide swath of the Midwest. However, there was a geographic epicenter of the Dust Bowl. Between 1930 and 1936 the hardest hit counties were in southwest Kansas and the panhandles of both Oklahoma and Texas.

Every farmhouse and small hamlet became a battle zone, as beleaguered residents fought the dust and wind. Historian William Manchester writes how "whole counties were transformed into shifting Saharas. Wives packed every windowsill, door frame, and keyhole with oiled cloth and gummed paper, yet the fine silt found its way in and lay in beach-like ripples on their floors."

Historian Donald Worster writes about these same difficulties:

> *Hospitals covered some of their patients with wet sheets, and housewives flapped the air with wet dishtowels to collect dust. One of the most common tactics was to stick masking tape, felt strips, or paraffin-soaked rags around the windows and door cracks. The typical plains house was loosely constructed and without insulation, but sometimes those methods proved so effective that there was not enough air circulation inside to replenish the oxygen supply... [P]eople simply had to open the window, dust or no dust... But most often there was no way to seal out the fine, blowing dirt: it blackened the pillow around one's head, the dinner plates on the table, the bread dough on the back of the stove. It became a steady part of one's diet and breathing.*

Farming Families Move Out

As the dust rolled in, farms were buried and farmers packed up their families and moved off the land. They became the dispossessed "Okies" and "Arkies" who loaded up their Dodge trucks and Ford Model-Ts and left their farms behind. Some were abandoning fields that their ancestors had claimed under the Homestead Act during the 1860s and 1870s. Altogether, between the Dust Bowl and the Depression, 350,000 Midwestern farmers fled their fields and headed for California.

6

End of the New Deal

With New Deal programs having fanned out in every direction to meet the challenges of the Great Depression, even those who were critical of various programs could not accuse FDR of having failed to put government power and resources to work. Millions of people had been put to work and direct relief had been applied from Wall Street to Main Street. In 1936 Democrats generally felt positive about the presidential election. At their convention, party delegates renominated Roosevelt.

THE ELECTION OF 1936

The Republicans had difficulty finding a candidate willing to take on the Goliath that FDR was obviously going to represent at the polls. They finally found one in Kansas—the simple, direct, yet boring Governor Alfred M. Landon. Landon was not exactly an opponent of the New Deal, as his moderate politics gave support to some of the New Deal programs. He was not, however, a fan of the Social Security Act. Throughout the campaign he and his fellow Republicans labeled the President as Franklin "Deficit" Roosevelt, whose administration had spent billions it didn't have, running up deficits on programs that were either wasteful, radical, experimental, or all three. The Democrats had proven themselves to be Socialists, cried former President Hoover, who characterized the Republican campaign as a "holy crusade for liberty."

Roosevelt, who loved political campaigning, met the accusations of the Republicans with vigor, even anger at times, referring to them as "economic royalists" who "hide behind the flag and the Constitution." Crowds cheered him on to November. The economy did seem to be improving. Banks were more solvent and secure. Social Security, while not having paid out a dime yet in benefits, seemed real to many—a promise waiting down the road. By the election unemployment had dipped below 14 percent, the lowest it had been since 1931. FDR was ready to serve another term, telling throngs of Americans:

> I should like to have it said of my first administration that in it the forces of selfishness and lust for power met their match. I should like to have it said of my second administration that in it these forces met their master.

Roosevelt's first term efforts paid off on election day, with 46 of the 48 states voting for the incumbent Democrat. Only Maine and Vermont (Calvin Coolidge's home state) went Republican. Electorally, the count was 523 to 8. The popular vote was less lopsided, with 27.7 million voting for FDR, while 16.7 million cast their ballots for the governor from the Sunflower state. Landon had not only been eclipsed by Roosevelt, he had failed to inspire. Someone joked, notes historian David Kennedy: "If Landon had given one more speech, Roosevelt would have carried Canada, too."

A NEW MANDATE

The president had staked everything, both personally and politically, on the New Deal. Through his efforts to meet the Depression, he had either retained or gained the support of

A banner for Franklin Delano Roosevelt and John Nance Garner for president and vice president for the 1936 presidential election. The photograph was taken in Harwick, Vermont, for the Farm Security Administration.

a wide variety of American groups. At its heart, perhaps, the 1936 election was a campaign based on class warfare. Labor unions, the poor, blacks, and leftists across the country had given their votes to keep FDR in the White House. Some, naturally, had voted for him because he had seen to their needs—a job, an income, some security, some hope. But the president had brought together a political war machine that had delivered victory.

Inauguration Day 1937 was a new day for the country, literally. The Twentieth Amendment to the Constitution, ratified in 1933, had moved the date for inaugurating presidents from March 4 to January 20. Some questioned the wisdom of this change when the weather turned nasty and Roosevelt took the oath of office against blustery, sleety winds. In his inaugural speech, he summed up his efforts over the previous four years: "Our progress out of the Depression is obvious." The president had a new mandate from the people, and he was eager to take on his next challenge.

THE COURT PACKING PLAN

Perhaps ironically, Roosevelt's next challenge would not be the Depression, but the United States Supreme Court. In seven decisions, the nation's top jurists had swept away several New Deal programs and various laws, including the NRA and AAA. FDR now prepared to meet the challenge of the conservative justices through a "court packing" scheme. He had become convinced through the elections of 1932, 1934, and 1936 that many of the nine men then serving as justices on the Court were out of touch with the nation; that their conservatism was out of date and that the Court's members, six of whom were over 70 years old, needed to get onboard with the nation (and his programs).

It was a simple plan: The president asked Congress to pass legislation allowing him to add additional justices to the

Supreme Court for every member over the age of 70, with a maximum membership of 15 justices. He claimed that the Court was so busy that its nine members could not keep up with their work, which was untrue. While FDR thought his new court idea would help streamline his work as President, it proved to be a terrible miscalculation. At its worst, the move looked like a power grab, especially to those who had already begun to think of FDR as a sort of self-styled dictator. The president's newest nickname was Franklin "Double-crossing" Roosevelt. Americans across the country, even many who had voted for him, were shocked at his blatant strategy to checkmate the power of the Court.

Congress did not cooperate with FDR, and the Court membership remained locked at nine. The president's aborted plan did have other results, however. Almost inexplicably, one of the conservative justices who had previously opposed New Deal acts, Owen J. Roberts, began voting in favor of FDR's programs as new cases reached the Court. The justices upheld the Wagner Act and the Social Security Act, as well as a state minimum wage law for women, having voted down another such law the previous year. Then, after Congress voted to offer full pay to any justice who retired after the age of 70, one of the oldest and most conservative justices retired, allowing Roosevelt to replace him with a New Deal supporter, Hugo Black.

Ultimately, FDR did manage to change the membership of the Supreme Court anyway. Due to deaths, resignations, and the fact that Roosevelt was president for 12 years in total, he eventually made nine new appointments to the high court.

THE NEW DEAL PETERS OUT

But Roosevelt's move in 1937 had another impact: Conservatives in Congress, both Republicans and Democrats, began to challenge additional New Deal legislation. The scope of the

New Deal had reached its highest level of reach and, despite FDR's great mandate represented by his 1936 victory, he had accomplished about all he was going to in his fight against the Great Depression. Historian David Kennedy notes: "Not with a bang, but a whimper, the New Deal petered out in 1938."

Yet the Depression had not been whipped by that year. In fact, during FDR's second term, several of the economic gains made during his first term began to fall apart. The nation's jobless rate had fallen by September 1937 to 5 million people, but that figure shot back up to 11 million by May 1938. On August 27, 1938 the stock market experienced another "Black Tuesday," with most stocks down between $2 and $15 per share—the largest drop in six years. Also, farm prices dropped after significant gains. Billions of federal dollars had been spent, but the gains to the economy, overall, had proven modest. As for the stock market, it was no better off than it had been in 1929. In fact, historian Amity Shlaes notes: "The Dow did not return to 1929 levels until nearly a decade after Roosevelt's death [in 1945]." In January 1938, unemployment in America was still hovering above 17 percent. Two years later, it had only dropped to 14.6. The chart on the opposite page presents the unemployment rate and the Dow Jones Average at various marking posts throughout the Depression.

The reversal of economic fortune was also making business leaders increasingly angry. As a group, they felt they had been blamed for the economy's downturn; were labeled as greedy; and were being taxed to the point of vengeance. The New Deal, they claimed, was pouring money at people who had little to add to the larger economy, while they were saddled with an encroaching government that thought it could run the economy better. To them, Roosevelt had proven to be not only aggressive, but nearly a dictator.

THE NEW DEAL: A STATISTICAL ANALYSIS

Date	Unemployment	Dow Jones Industrial Average
July 1927	3.3%	168
October 1929	5.0%	343 (October 1)
		230 (October 29)
September 1931	17.4%	140
October 1933	22.9%	93
November 1933	23.2%	90
January 1934	21.2%	100
November 1934	23.2%	93
July 1935	21.3%	119
December 1936	15.3%	182
January 1937	15.1%	179
August 1937	13.5%	187
January 1938	17.4%	121
January 1940	14.6%	151

A DIMINISHED LEGACY

The New Deal, in time, became a shadow of its former self. By 1943, the heart was removed from the aging and increasingly irrelevant New Deal. When the 78th Congress came into session following the 1942 elections, they began to dismantle several longstanding programs, including the National Youth Administration, the Works Progress Administration, and the youth-oriented, faithful servant of conservation, the Civilian Conservation Corps. With full employment brought on by manufacturing and the supplying of food and resources for World War II, such programs were no longer needed. The Farm Security Administration and the Rural Electrification Administration, which had brought great social change, lost nearly all their federal funding.

The New Deal: Hero or Villian?

Critics at the time and some historians today criticize President Franklin Delano Roosevelt for his tendency to use the power of the federal government to intervene constantly in the nation's economy. They point to wasteful spending on programs that did not work and the fragmentary nature of the New Deal, which sometimes seemed to lack cohesion, single-minded purpose, and clear direction.

Sometimes FDR's intervention may indeed have been damaging to the economy. Even Hoover, who remained conservative concerning government meddling, made mistakes. He worked to push wages upward when the natural tendency at the time was for them to drop. He stuck with the disastrous Smoot-Hawley Tariff and allowed it to become law, which hurt America's position as an international trade power. Hoover raised taxes late in his term, when few could begin to afford it. Through such errors, U.S. industry continued to suffer after 1932, even as such industrialized nations as Japan, Sweden, New Zealand, Greece, Romania, Denmark, Chile, and Finland were seeing recovery.

When Roosevelt entered the White House, he unleashed federal power, relying on his New Deal programs and agencies to regulate various aspects of the economy—industrial output, small businesses, banks, monetary policy—while providing safety nets of aid and relief to various groups considered in need. He approached this strategy with the belief that the government needed to mobilize as if going to war, with the Depression as the enemy. Some programs were efficient, effective, even inspiring, such as the Civil Conservation Corps or banking reform. The results included denting unemployment and stabilizing parts of the economy.

But other New Deal programs were destructive. The NRA was misplaced, its rules and codes so narrowly defined and restrictive that businesses were ultimately hurt. Employers hated to hire under the NRA, and the program kept many from investing in new businesses or expanding their operations. Part of the problem was that when a program like the NRA was established, the laws that created it were so vague that they were open to extreme interpretation. Economic growth was stymied. Other New Deal programs, such as the Tennessee Valley Authority, pushed out capitalistic investment by the private sector. By the same token, Roosevelt pushed higher taxes on the business community, such as the undistributed profits tax, taking potential investment capital out of their hands.

Another criticism of the New Deal, both then and now, was the level of socialism inherent in some of its programs and among its very designers and architects. Some of Roosevelt's advisors—those who made up his "Brain Trust"—seemed too radical, including among their ranks leftist professors and socialist economists.

As already noted in this book, FDR, despite accusations of radicalism from conservatives, had not engaged in true revolution, but had initiated bold reforms without resorting to the barrel of a gun. The 1930s delivered a host of dictators of all stripes, from Europe to Asia—Fascists, Communists, strident Socialists, and militaristic warlords. In the end, the New Deal did not end the Depression or destroy U.S. democracy. And Roosevelt had remained, at his core, a capitalist.

That same government spent $20 billion in six years—a sum equivalent today to half a trillion dollars. In the meantime the national debt had skyrocketed thanks to FDR's application of Keynesian economics (deficit spending), from a gigantic $19.5 billion in 1932 to an astronomical $40 billion by 1939. (These numbers, however, would soon be dwarfed by the high level of government spending during World War II.) Money had been thrown at problem after problem, creating an artificial economy based on government-financed work programs, only to see those same problems continue. Meanwhile industry struggled along, unable to close the gap between what to produce and what consumers were willing or able to buy. Ultimately, the nation's economy and its sluggish unemployment problem would have to wait until World War II to be solved.

Some programs of the New Deal did remain however, and are still a part of the social fabric of the United States today, such as Social Security and the Federal Deposit Insurance Corporation (FDIC).

The war was on by the late 1930s, and the Great Depression receded ever into the past. At a press conference held on December 28, 1943, Roosevelt took the opportunity to address the New Deal he had created to rescue America from its worst economic nightmares. His words explained what everyone who had experienced the Depression already knew: "How did the New Deal come into existence? It was because there was an awfully sick patient called the United States of America, and it was suffering from a grave internal disorder... And they sent for the doctor." Roosevelt had helped to save the nation's banking system, salvage the country's farms, repair America's securities markets, put Americans back to work, carry out countless conservation projects, build dams and highways and airports and bridges, and bring a greater level of security to America's aged. The New Deal had served all those purposes, even if not perfectly, during America's greatest time of economic need and uncertainty.

7

American Culture of the 1930s

The Great Depression of the 1930s brought difficult economic times for tens of millions of Americans. Even for people who were fortunate enough to keep their jobs, have homes to live in, and be able to put food on the table, the times were still challenging. Many of those who lived through the Depression relied on the popular culture of the era to provide a distraction from the misery of daily life.

KEEPING AMERICA'S VALUES

One concern among many Americans was that the nation's values might experience dramatic, negative change as a result of the Depression. For some it did. There was a handful of lawless individuals—from bank robbers and cop killers, such as Bonnie and Clyde and Babyface Nelson, to gangsters like John Dillinger—who responded to the challenge of the Depression by turning to crime and murder. But the vast majority of Americans remained true to the nation's overall moral values of honesty, hard work, and individual responsibility.

One might have expected many Americans to have become cynical during the Depression, seeing themselves as little more than the helpless victims of such big money fat cats as Wall Street moguls, remote heads of corporations, and greedy bankers. Yet the vast majority of the country's citizens chose to commit themselves to the future, when the economy might turn around and prosperity and personal potential might gain another shot at the brass ring. Many were too proud to accept direct relief, preferring work instead of charity.

THE SMALL SET

Another value that many Americans clung to was their optimism and hope for the future. One means of coping through the bad times was to listen to the relatively new medium of radio. Radio had been becoming more popular in the mid-1920s, but the numbers of radio listeners mushroomed dramatically during the Great Depression. Just like television sets today, in the 1930s nearly every family in America had at least one radio at home. From farmhouse parlors to the living rooms of brownstones in major cities across the country, Americans tuned in to their radios and listened to an increasingly wide variety of programs. For many, the radio was a shared social experience. People might gather on a neighbor's front porch and listen to a national broadcast or a local program. They could also tune in to national sporting events and local ball play.

America's airwaves were filled with a host of entertaining shows, music, dramas, comedies, news programs, and cultural events. The Thirties marked the beginning of the great era of the radio serials, programs that broadcast each week at a scheduled time slot across the nation. Daytime programming catered to women working in their homes, and included drama and romance serials. During the evenings, radio schedules featured news broadcasts, comic shows, and variety hours. The supper hours were given over to children's programming mostly, with a typical line up that might include the following:

> *5:15 WTIC 1040 Tom Mix*
> *WEAF 660 Story Man*
> *5:30 WTIC 1040 Jack Armstrong*
> *WJZ 760 Singing Lady*
> *5:45 WJZ 760 Little Orphan Annie*
> *WOR 710 Uncle Don*

Popular radio programs of the period included the crime fighting "Green Hornet," "Ripley's Believe it or Not!," the vine-swinging "Tarzan," the square-jawed "Dick Tracy," and super-duper spaceman, "Buck Rogers in the 25th Century." When Macy's department store in New York announced Buck Rogers Disintegrator Guns for sale, 20,000 people lined up outside the store.

THE BIG SCREEN

For many Americans who sought entertainment outside the home, the national medium was motion pictures. By the end of the 1930s, nearly two out of every three Americans—80 million people—attended the movies at least once a week, with adults usually paying 25 cents a ticket and children, 10 cents. Film became the common entertainment outlet for people seeking a respite from the difficulties and challenges of daily life during the Depression.

While motion pictures had existed for 30 years by the time FDR became president, films with synchronized sound had only been around for a few years. The 1930s became an innovative and ground-breaking decade for the film industry, and the variety of motion pictures was wide, even if the content was typically censored.

Some films made social commentary, while others were nothing more than distracting comedies, or period-set dramatic productions on a grand scale. John Steinbeck's popular Depression-era novel, *The Grapes of Wrath*, reached the big screen in 1940, with Henry Fonda in the lead role as Tom Joad. Director Frank Capra produced such populist-themed films as *Mr. Deeds Goes to Town* (1936) and *Mr. Smith Goes to Washington* (1939), featuring actor Jimmy Stewart as a newly elected, naïve senator fighting corruption in the nation's capitol.

Historical epics were popular, with their elaborate period stage sets. They included *Mutiny on the Bounty,* starring the decade's heart-throb, Clark Gable; Errol Flynn and Bette Davis in *The Private Lives of Elizabeth and Essex;* and the grande dame film of the decade, set during the Civil War, *Gone With the Wind,* starring Vivian Leigh and Clark Gable.

Laughter and Screams

Comedies were commonplace, because Americans badly needed something to laugh at. The Marx Brothers appeared in screwball films such as *Animal Crackers* (1930), *Horse Feathers* (1932) and *A Night at the Opera* (1935), some of which were little more than film versions of their vaudeville stage shows. Other favorite screen comedians included W. C. Fields, the comic team of Laurel and Hardy, and wide-mouthed Joe E. Brown. For kids, there were the *Bowery Boys* and *Our Gang* series, which included the likes of Spanky, Weezer, Alfalfa, and Buckwheat, a black character. Child actors of the era included sausage-curled Shirley Temple and everyone's favorite, all-American teen, Andy Hardy, played by Mickey Rooney.

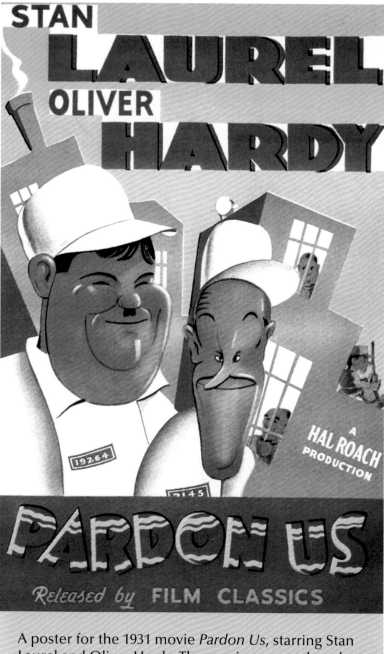

A poster for the 1931 movie *Pardon Us*, starring Stan
Laurel and Oliver Hardy. The movie was produced
by Hal Roach Sr., who went on to be one of the most
successful film and television producers to date.

There were horror films, including *Dracula* and *Franken-stein,* both released in 1931, followed by *King Kong* (1933), which featured a variety of crude special effects. Another popular subject matter for 1930s films were the gangsters of the era, including *Public Enemy* (1931) and *Little Caesar* (1930), which featured such stars as James Cagney and Edward G. Robinson, both of whom would still be making films into the 1970s and 1980s. These films were usually made under the stark limitations of black and white. They were juxtaposed against the heavily choreographed musicals of the 1930s, including elaborate stage productions by Busby Berkeley, such as *Gold Diggers of 1933,* which featured hosts of leggy chorus girls.

Walt Disney

Perhaps more significant as a trend in film during the 1930s was the animation produced by Midwestern artist Walt Disney. Disney began his career making crude animations in Kansas City for local advertisers, but moved to Hollywood to produce animated shorts for movie houses. His first was *Oswald the Lucky Rabbit* (1927), followed by the original Mickey Mouse cartoon, *Steamboat Willie* (1928). More Disney animated shorts followed through the 1930s, in color, rather than the early black and white, but Disney changed the animation industry forever when, in 1937, he released his first feature length animated film, *Snow White and the Seven Dwarfs.* It soon became a classic.

MAGAZINES OF THE 1930s

Despite the popularity of radio during the 1930s, print media became even more popular than ever. Even in the midst of the Depression, new magazines and journals were launched. The first issues of the photographic journal, *Life,* reached the newsstands in 1936, for example. The cover of its first issue

"RED-BLOODED" AMERICANS

The Roosevelt administration met with constant criticism for its extensive use of the power of the U.S. federal government. FDR and his administrators did not ultimately abandon capitalism, but rather tweaked it a little. Yet radicalism was a part of the U.S. landscape during the Thirties. One of the signs of this was a rising membership in the American Communist Party.

Leading the way in this trend was the Popular Front, a combination of political groups across the country that were anti-fascist, as well as anti-capitalist. With support from Stalin and the Soviet Union, the Popular Front began praising FDR and his handling of the Depression. They tried to sway the minds of many Americans by adopting the slogan, "Communism is twentieth-century Americanism." Under the organization's influence, membership in the American Communist Party increased to 100,000 by the mid-1930s.

Many intellectuals began taking the Communist Party seriously. When civil war erupted in Spain, with Fascists fighting to take over the government, 3,000 young Americans, many of them Communists, went to Spain to fight. The Communist Party organized rallies for the unemployed and a hunger march in Washington, D.C. in 1931. Union organizers were sometimes members of the American Communist Party. They even tried to organize a union of black sharecroppers in Alabama.

Yet the American Communist Party was not a truly "American" institution. It had strong ties with Moscow, and American members were closely supervised by the Russians. This became clear in 1939, when the Soviet leader, Josef Stalin, signed an agreement with Germany's fascist leader, Adolf Hitler, under which both nations agreed not to attack one another. Following this, Communist leaders in Moscow ordered the American Communist Party to shut down the Popular Front and begin campaigning against the liberalism of the New Deal. This move puzzled and angered American Communist Party regulars, many of whom left the party, disillusioned. U.S. radicalism was struck a hard blow.

featured a photo by Margaret Bourke-White of a New Deal-era hydroelectric dam. For decades, *Life* would be one of the nation's most popular magazines. Popular weekly, biweekly, or monthly magazines of the decade included *Collier's, Look, McCall's Photoplay, The Catholic Digest, The Atlantic, The New Yorker, Redbook*, and the most widely read of them all, *Reader's Digest*. There were magazines for every taste and interest: *Screenland* and *Silver Screen* for moviegoers; *Time*, a no-nonsense news magazine; and those for the simplest of tastes, including *Cowboy Short Stories, Sweetheart Stories, Detective Story, Astounding Science Fiction, Ace Sports, Crackerjack Funnies*, and *College Humor.*

A NEW LITERATURE

Just as the 1920s had produced a new era of serious writers, so the decade of the Depression did as well. Many of those who had written before the stock market crashed had focused on the materialism of the Twenties. The new literature of the Thirties did not fall prey to the economic despair of the era, but took on the voice of social conscience. John Dos Passos's *U.S.A.* trilogy (1930–36) continued the earlier literary focus on America's obsession with material wealth. Some authors wrote of a coming revolution in the United States, with writer F. Scott Fitzgerald even suggesting that Communism might hold the answers for the country's future. But much of that movement lost its steam and drive as reports emerged from the Soviet Union of the harsh control exerted by Josef Stalin and the brutal murders of tens of thousands of his opponents.

Steinbeck and Wright

Two writers whose works spoke on behalf of social justice and change were John Steinbeck and Richard Wright. Perhaps no writer of the era captured the grip of the Depression on the American heart and soul better than Steinbeck, who published four novels during the 1930s—*Tortilla Flat* (1935), *In Dubious Battle* (1936), *Of Mice and Men* (1937), and *The Grapes of Wrath* (1939). This story follows the difficulties of the Joad family as they abandon their dusted out farm in Oklahoma and head west along Route 66,

A still image from *The Wizard of Oz*, a musical-fantasy movie made in 1939. The movie was based on a children's novel written by L. Frank Baum in 1900.

lured by visions of a California paradise where jobs and fruit abound. Throughout the novel, the Joad family is battered to the point of collapse, illustrating Steinbeck's belief that the working class was downtrodden and would only survive through organization and radicalism.

Black writer Richard Wright was born on a plantation outside Natchez, Mississippi, and grew up with an insatiable appetite for books. A white friend checked out books for him from a segregated public library in Memphis. As a young man in his twenties, Wright moved to Chicago and soon found work with the Federal Writers' Project. Between 1934 and 1944, he was a member of the Communist Party, but he eventually renounced the party. His greatest published work was *Native Son* (1940), a novel that presented a black protagonist, Bigger Thomas, born in a ghetto. Bigger flirts with Communism, but is never fully accepted by his comrades in the organization. He descends into psychological confusion until he accidentally murders his employer's daughter. Hounded by a mob, Bigger kills his girlfriend, is captured, and condemned to die. Wright's novel is written with rage and bitterness, noted in the words of Bigger: "They wouldn't let me live and so I killed."

Wolfe and Faulkner

The Thirties produced several additional Southern writers of significance, including Thomas Wolfe and William Faulkner. Wolfe's most important work was his novel *Look Homeward, Angel* (1929), which was a semi-autobiographical telling of his North Carolina youth, including his college experiences at Chapel Hill (called "Pulpit Hill" in the book). His character, Eugene Grant, searches for his own identity and emerges from his experiences having broken away from his family's drab life and found his own path. Grant has discovered, in Wolfe's words, "You can't go home again."

Mississippi writer William Faulkner penned several novels during the era, beginning with *Sartoris* (1929), which set the stage for much of Faulkner's later works, largely set in his fictional Mississippi county, Yoknapatawpha. He followed up with *The Sound and the Fury* (1929), *As I Lay Dying* (1930), *Light in August* (1932), and *Absalom! Absalom!* (1936). Faulkner's work presented the foibles and sins of Southern history, creating a style that destined him to be one of the great modern writers of the twentieth century.

A NEW BATTLE APPROACHES

By the end of the 1930s the United States had experienced at least ten years of hard times, unemployment, radical change in the role of the federal government in the lives of many of its citizens, and great shifts in its popular culture. FDR had overseen the New Deal, which had battled the Depression at every turn, with mixed results. But there was a new challenge on the horizon.

The world stage was becoming crowded with extremist leaders: the Spanish Fascist Francisco Franco; Italy's socialist blowhard Benito Mussolini; warlords in Japan; and the German Führer, National Socialist Adolf Hitler. Their armies were on the march, and the threats they represented to the democratic nations of the world now appeared as real as the Great Depression had seemed to so many throughout the decade. A new battle was approaching, and the U.S. war on poverty, unemployment, and corporate greed was about to give way to the greatest conflagration of war in the history of the world.

Chronology

1929 Throughout the year, more than 600 U.S. banks close their doors

March 4 Herbert Hoover is inaugurated as President of the United States

September Dow Jones Industrial Index reaches a high of 452

October 24 "Black Thursday": 13 million shares of stock change hands

TIMELINE

1929
Throughout the year, more than 600 U.S. banks close their doors

1929
October 24: "Black Thursday"—13 million shares of stock change hands

1931
Throughout the year, 2,000 U.S. banks close their doors

1933
February 15: A gunman attempts to assassinate Roosevelt

1933
March 4: Roosevelt is inaugurated as President

1929	1930	1931	1932	1933

1929
October 29: "Black Tuesday"—16 million shares are traded, and the Dow Jones Industrial Average drops 43 points

1931
September: U.S. unemployment rate is 17.4 percent and Dow Jones Industrial Average stands at 140

1932
July: Dow Jones Industrial Index hits bottom of 58

1933
October: U.S. unemployment rate is 22.9 percent and Dow Jones Industrial Average stands at 93

October 29 "Black Tuesday": 16 million shares are traded, and the Dow Jones Industrial Average drops 43 points

1930 Throughout the year, more than 1,000 U.S. banks close their doors

June 17 President Hoover signs the Smoot-Hawley Tariff Act, raising U.S. tariffs to the highest levels ever

1931 Throughout the year, 2,000 U.S. banks close their doors

September The U.S. unemployment rate reaches 17.4 percent and Dow Jones Industrial Average stands at 140

1932

February 2 The Reconstruction Finance Corporation is opened for business

1934
January 31: Roosevelt returns the dollar to the gold standard

1935
May 6: FDR establishes the Works Progress Administration (WPA)

May 27: U.S. Supreme Court declares the National Industrial Recovery Act unconstitutional

1936
November 3: FDR wins a seond term, defeating the Republican Alf Landon of Kansas, and taking 46 of 48 states

1938
June: FDR signs the Fair Labor Standards Act, establishing a minimum wage and maximum work hours

1934   **1935**   **1936**   **1937**   **1938**

1934
January: U.S. unemployment rate is 21.2 percent and Dow Jones Industrial Average stands at 100

1935
July: U.S. unemployment rate is 21.3 percent and Dow Jones Industrial Average stands at 119

1937
January: U.S. unemployment rate is 15.1 percent and Dow Jones Industrial Average stands at 179

1938
January: U.S. unemployment rate is 17.4 percent and Dow Jones Industrial Average stands at 121

April 7 FDR delivers a radio speech, stating he is campaigning for the "forgotten man at the bottom of the economic pyramid"

May The Bonus Marchers arrive in Washington, D.C. seeking their early combined pension and life insurance payments

July Dow Jones Industrial Index hits bottom of 58

July 28 Hoover orders the removal of the Bonus Marchers from their shanties at Anacostia Flats

November 8 Franklin Roosevelt is elected President of the United States

1933

February 15 A gunman attempts to assassinate Roosevelt but shoots Chicago Mayor Anton Cermak instead

February 20 Congress proposes the Twenty-First Amendment to end Prohibition

March 4 Roosevelt is inaugurated as President

March 5 FDR orders a four-day bank holiday, which ends all bank transactions

March 9 Roosevelt begins his first "Hundred Days," during which his New Deal takes shape. The Emergency Banking Bill is sent to Congress and passed later that same day

March 12 Roosevelt delivers the first of his "Fireside Chat" radio broadcasts

March 31 Congress passes the Reforestation Relief Act, which creates the Civilian Conservation Corps (CCC).

April 19 FDR announces that the United States will abandon the gold standard, lowering the value of the dollar overseas

May 18 Congress passes a bill creating the Tennessee Valley Authority

May 19 Roosevelt appoints Harry Hopkins to head the Federal Emergency Relief Administration. Later

that month, Congress creates the Agricultural
Adjustment Administration (AAA)

May 27 Roosevelt signs the Securities Act of 1933

June 16 Marking the end of the "Hundred Days,"
Congress passes the Farm Credit Act, the Banking
Act of 1933 (which establishes the Federal Deposit
Insurance Corporation), and the National Industry
Recovery Act (which creates the National Industry
Recovery Administration and the Public Works
Administration)

August 5 Roosevelt establishes the National Labor
Board

October U.S. unemployment rate is 22.9 percent and
Dow Jones Industrial Average stands at 93

November The Civil Works Administration is
established

December 29 Dow Jones Industrial Average closes the
year at 99

1934

January 31 Roosevelt returns the dollar to the gold
standard and signs the Farm Mortgage Refinancing
Act. The U.S. unemployment rate is 21.2 percent
and Dow Jones Industrial Average stands at 100

April 27 Roosevelt signs amendment to Home Owners
Loan Act of 1933

May 28 British economist John Maynard Keynes meets
with FDR

June 6 FDR signs the Securities and Exchange Act,
which establishes the Securities and Exchange
Commission

June 12 Roosevelt signs Reciprocal Trade Agreement
Act, allowing him to lower tariffs by 50 percent

June 19 FDR signs Communications Act, establishing
the Federal Communications Commission

June 28 Roosevelt signs the National Housing Act, which establishes the Federal Housing Administration

November 6 Democrats win significant gains in both houses of Congress. U.S. unemployment rate is 22.9 percent and Dow Jones Industrial Average stands at 93

1935

April 27 Roosevelt signs bill to create the Soil Conservation Service within the U.S. Department of Agriculture

May 6 FDR establishes the Works Progress Administration (WPA)

May 11 FDR establishes the Rural Electrification Administration

May 27 U.S. Supreme Court rules in the *Schechter Poultry Corp. v. United States* case and declares the National Industrial Recovery Act unconstitutional

July 5 FDR signs the Wagner Act, establishing the National Labor Relations Board. U.S. unemployment rate is 21.3 percent and Dow Jones Industrial Average stands at 119

August 14 Social Security Act becomes law

1936

January 6 Supreme Court rules that the Agricultural Adjustment Act is unconstitutional

February 17 Supreme Court upholds Tennessee Valley Authority

November 3 FDR wins a seond term, defeating the Republican Alf Landon of Kansas, and taking 46 of 48 states

December U.S. unemployment rate is 15.3 percent and Dow Jones Industrial Average stands at 182

1937

January 20 Roosevelt's second inauguration. U.S. unemployment rate is 15.1 percent and Dow Jones Industrial Average stands at 179

February 5 FDR announces his Supreme Court packing scheme in the form of the Federal Court Reorganization bill, which is not passed

August U.S. unemployment rate is 13.5 percent and Dow Jones Industrial Average stands at 187

December Autoworkers engage in "sit down" strikes at General Motors plants

1938

January U.S. unemployment rate is 17.4 percent and Dow Jones Industrial Average stands at 121

June 25 FDR signs the Fair Labor Standards Act, establishing a minimum wage and maximum work hours

Glossary

Agricultural Adjustment Act (AAA) An agency created by Congress in 1933, during FDR's Hundred Days, to help destitute farmers.

"Arkies" Uprooted farmers from Arkansas who migrated across the country in search of work.

Black Thursday October 24, 1929, the day the stock market witnessed 13 million shares traded, and $9 billion no longer invested in the market. This was a signal of significant trouble for the economy.

Black Tuesday October 29, 1929, the day the stock market dropped by 43 points.

Bonus Army Veterans of World War I who marched on Washington, D.C. in 1932 and again in 1933. They were seeking the early payment of their bonuses, which were not due to be paid until 1945.

Brain Trust A group of close advisors of President Franklin D. Roosevelt during the early days of his first term. Their policy suggestions helped to mold much of the New Deal legislation.

broker The person through whom a stock investor makes his or her stock purchase.

Civilian Conservation Corps The New Deal program created in 1933 that put boys and young men to work planting trees and making general improvements in the nation's parks.

Court-packing plan An attempt made by President Roosevelt in 1937 to increase his power over the Supreme Court. He tried to push legislation through

Congress authorizing him to add additional justices to the Supreme Court. The plan was refused.

Crash of 1929 The massive crash of the U.S. stock market on "Black Tuesday," when investors sold more than 16 million shares of stock in one day.

Dust Bowl A large area of the Midwest that suffered from recurring violent dust storms and drought during the 1930s.

Fireside Chats A series of weekly radio addresses to the American people delivered by President Roosevelt, during which he explained what actions he had recently taken to fight the Depression.

Hooverville A derisive name given to shantytowns that sprang up in the early years of the Depression and were occupied by migrants in search of jobs. They were named after Herbert Hoover, the president of the time.

The Hundred Days President Roosevelt's first 100 days in office, in the spring and early summer of 1932. During this period Congress passed 15 major bills that reshaped the U.S. economy.

margin buying A practice of purchasing stock through a broker that was common in the 1920s. It allowed the investor to buy a portion of stock on credit, with the broker carrying the debt.

National Industrial Recovery Act The New Deal act passed during FDR's "100 Days" that was intended to drive up prices and provide jobs. The act created the National Recovery Administration and the Public Works Administration.

National Recovery Administration Part of the National Industrial Recovery Act, the NRA was created to solve problems of economic instability, overproduction, and labor-management issues by carrying out economic planning through "codes" of competition.

New Deal The collection of agencies, laws, and administrative structures created by the Roosevelt administration which were designed to meet the challenges of the Depression by expanding the role of government in the economy, including the private sector, while providing direct relief and job programs to Americans.

"Okies" Uprooted farmers from Oklahoma who migrated across the country in search of work.

parity The prices farmers received for their produce, relative to industrial prices as they had stood just prior to World War I in 1914.

Public Works Administration Part of the National Industrial Recovery Act, this agency oversaw public works projects that included new transportation facilities, hospitals, and public buildings.

reparations Compensation payable to the victor by a nation defeated in war, especially the payments demanded of Germany after World War I.

Second Hundred Days President Roosevelt's second batch of New Deal proposals and programs, created in 1935. They included the Wagner Act, Social Security, the Rural Electrification Act, a stronger Federal Reserve Board, the National Youth Administration, and the Soil Conservation Act.

Social Security A government program created in August 1935 and designed to provide a retirement fund for the elderly, unemployed insurance, and welfare grants for local distribution.

Southern Renaissance An influential group of Southern writers, including William Faulkner and Tom Wolfe, who spawned a new style of fiction during the 1930s, based on realism and other modern influences.

subsidy A government payment made to farmers to increase their income.

Tennessee Valley Authority A government agency created to help the Tennessee River Valley with water management and flood control, and to provide hydroelectric power through the construction of water projects and dams.

Twentieth Amendment A constitutional amendment which changed the date of an incoming president's inauguration from March 4 to January 20. FDR's second inauguration, in 1937, was the first one to take place on the new date.

Twenty-First Amendment A constitutional amendment, ratified in 1933, which repealed the Eighteenth Amendment and thus ended Prohibition.

Works Progress (Projects) Administration A government agency created in January 1935 through which workers were hired for "light construction" projects, especially those related to the arts.

Bibliography

Alter, Jonathan. *The Defining Moment: FDR's Hundred Days and the Triumph of Hope.* New York: Simon & Schuster Paperbacks, 2006.

Brands, H. W. *Traitor to His Class: The Privileged Life and Radical Presidency of Franklin Delano Roosevelt.* New York: Doubleday, 2008.

Cohen, Adam. *Nothing to Fear: FDR's Inner Circle and the Hundred Days That Created Modern America.* New York: The Penguin Press, 2009.

Doak, Robin Santos. *Black Tuesday.* Mankato, MN: Capstone Press, Inc., 2007.

Dulles, Rhea Foster, and Melvyn Dubofsky. *Labor in America: A History.* Arlington Heights, IL: Harlan Davidson, 1984.

Hamilton, David E. *Problems in American Civilization: The New Deal.* Boston: Cengage Learning (Wadsworth), 1998.

Hart, James D. *The Oxford Companion to American Literature.* New York: Oxford University Press, 1983.

Heilbroner, Robert. *The Economic Transformation of America, 1600 to the Present.* Fort Worth: Harcourt Brace College Publishers, 1994.

Horowitz, David A. *On the Edge: The U.S. in the 20th Century.* Belmont, CA: West / Wadsworth, 1998.

Kennedy, David. *Freedom From Fear: The American People in Depression and War, 1929–1945.* New York: Oxford University Press, 1999.

Manchester, William. *The Glory and the Dream: A Narrative History of America, 1932–1972.* Boston: Little, Brown & Company, 1973.

Martin, James Kirby. *America and Its People,* 2nd edition. New York: HarperCollins Publishers, 1993

Remini, Robert V. *A Short History of the United States.* New York: HarperCollins Publishers, 2008.

Shlaes, Amity. *The Forgotten Man: A New History of the Great Depression.* New York: HarperCollins Publishers, 2007.

Smith, Carter. *Presidents: Every Question Answered.* New York: Metro Books, 2004.

Steinbeck, John. *The Grapes of Wrath.* New York: Viking Press, 1939.

Sunstein, Cass R. *The Second Bill of Rights: FDR's Unfinished Revolution and Why We Need it More Than Ever.* New York: Perseus Publishing, 2006.

Taylor, Nick. *American-Made: The Enduring Legacy of the WPA: When FDR Put the Nation to Work.* New York: Bantam Books, 2008.

Tindall, George Brown and David Emory Shi. *America: A Narrative History.* New York: W. W. Norton & Company, 1997.

Wecter, Dixon. *The Age of the Great Depression, 1929–1941.* New York: Macmillan Publishing, 1948.

Weinstein, Allen. *The Story of America: Freedom and Crisis From Settlement to Superpower.* New York: DK Publishing, Inc., 2002.

Wolfe, Thomas. *Look Homeward, Angel.* New York: Simon & Schuster Adult Publishing Group, 2006.

Worster, Donald. *Dust Bowl: The Southern Plains in the 1930s.* New York: Oxford University Press, 2004. (25th Anniversary Edition.)

Further Resources

Burg, David F. *The Great Depression.* New York: Facts on File, Inc., 2005.

Downing, David. *Great Depression.* Portsmouth, NH: Heinemann Library, 2001.

Elish, Dan. *Franklin Delano Roosevelt.* Tarrytown, NY: Marshall Cavendish, Inc., 2008.

Feinberg, Barbara Silberdick. *Franklin D. Roosevelt.* New York: Scholastic Library Publishing, 2005.

Fitzgerald, Stephanie. *The New Deal: Rebuilding America.* Mankato, MN: Capstone Press, Inc., 2006.

Freedman, Russell. *Children of the Great Depression.* New York: Houghton Mifflin Harcourt, 2006.

————. *Franklin Delano Roosevelt.* New York: Houghton Mifflin Harcourt, 1992.

Grant, R. G. *The Great Depression.* Farmington Hills, MI: Cengage Gale, 2005.

Hillstrom, Kevin. *The Great Depression and the New Deal.* Detroit: Omnigraphics, Inc., 2008.

Landau, Elaine. *The Great Depression.* San Francisco: Children's Press, 2007.

Levinson, Jeff. *Great Depression: A Nation in Distress.* Orlando, FL: Discovery Enterprises, Limited, 1996.

Mara, Wil. *Franklin D. Roosevelt.* San Francisco: Children's Press, 2004.

Meyers, Madeleine. *Great Depression.* Hoboken, NJ: History Compass, 2000.

Nardo, Don. *Great Depression.* Farmington Hills, MI: Cengage Gale, Greenhaven Press, 2007.

Woog, Adam. *Roosevelt and the New Deal.* Farmington Hills, MI: Cengage Gale, 1997.

Web sites

Franklin Delano Roosevelt:
   http://www.whitehouse.gov/about/presidents/
      franklindroosevelt/
   http://www.fdrlibrary.marist.edu/
   http://www.youtube.com/watch?v=MX_v0zxM23Q
      (Film of FDR's first inauguration)
   http://www.youtube.com/watch?v=jt9f-MZX-58
      (Recording of FDR's first "Fireside Chat," March 12, 1933)

The Civilian Conservation Corps:
   http://www.youtube.com/watch?v=H72vxNFjzSQ
      (Film of Washington State Parks Civilian Conservation
      Corps)

The Depression:
   http://www.english.illinois.edu/maps/depression/about.htm
   http://history1900s.about.com/library/photos/blyindex
      depression.htm
   http://www.memory.loc.gov/ammem/fsachtml/
   http://www.amatecon.com/greatdepression.html
   http://www.youtube.com/watch?v=2jvbTwxdbvE
      (Still photos and music of the Depression)

The Dust Bowl:
   http://www.pbs.org/wgbh/americanexperience/dustbowl/
   http://www.ccccok.org/museum/dustbowl.html

The New Deal:
   http://newdeal.feri.org/
   http://iws.ccccd.edu/kwilkison/Online1302home/
      20th%20Century/DepressionNewDeal.html

The Work Projects Administration:
   http://www.youtube.com/watch?v=Gk0SpTOi9Aw&feature=
      related
      (Archival film of WPA)
   http://www.youtube.com/watch?v=Umxfo4eLOnM
      (Archival film of WPA)

Picture Credits

Index

About the Author

Tim McNeese is associate professor of history at York College in York, Nebraska. Professor McNeese holds degrees from York College, Harding University, and Missouri State University. He has published more than 100 books and educational materials. His writing has earned him a citation in the library reference work, *Contemporary Authors* and multiple citations in *Best Books for Young Teen Readers*. In 2006, Tim appeared on the History Channel program, *Risk Takers, History Makers: John Wesley Powell and the Grand Canyon*. He was been a faculty member at the Tony Hillerman Writers Conference in Albuquerque. His wife, Beverly, is assistant professor of English at York College. They have two married children, Noah and Summer, and four grandchildren—Ethan, Adrianna, Finn William, and Ari. Tim and Bev have sponsored college study trips on the Lewis and Clark Trail, to the American Southwest, and to New England. You may contact Professor McNeese at tdmcneese@york.edu.

About the Consultant

Richard Jensen is Research Professor at Montana State University, Billings. He has published 11 books on a wide range of topics in American political, social, military, and economic history, as well as computer methods. After taking a Ph.D. at Yale in 1966, he taught at numerous universities, including Washington, Michigan, Harvard, Illinois-Chicago, West Point, and Moscow State University in Russia.